LEVI'S & LACE

LEVI'S & LACE

ARIZONA WOMEN WHO MADE HISTORY

BY JAN CLEERE

RIO NUEVO PUBLISHERS

Rio Nuevo Publishers®
P. O. Box 5250
Tucson, AZ 85703-0250
(520) 623-9558
www.rionuevo.com

Library of Congress Cataloging-in-Publication Data

Cleere, Jan.
  Levi's & lace : Arizona women who made history / Jan Cleere.
    p. cm.
  Includes bibliographical references.
  ISBN-13: 978-1-933855-53-0 (pbk. : alk. paper)
  ISBN-10: 1-933855-53-3 (pbk. : alk. paper)
  1. Women--Arizona--Biography. 2. Women--Arizona--History.
  3. Arizona--Biography. 4. Arizona--History.
  I. Title. II. Title: Levi's and lace.
  CT3262.A6C55 2011
  920.7209791--dc22
                    2010050296

10 9 8 7 6 5 4 3 2 1

*To Kevin, Rebecca,
Kristopher, and Vivien.*

*Through the unity of family
we make our greatest strides.*

CONTENTS

WOMEN OF THE ARTS

WOMEN OF THE LAW

And This Is Life

And this is life—to have and hold
A little love, a little gold;
To prove the Dream with work well done;
To rest an hour before the sun
Drops down to night—then journey on
An unmapped road to see the Dawn.

—SHARLOT HALL, 1911
Cactus and Pine:
Songs of the Southwest

INTRODUCTION

The women in this book, though they may not be the most famous Arizona women, all made their mark on the early history of Arizona as it became a territory and young state. They were selected for their fortitude in the face of adversity, their confrontation of extraordinary and sometimes-dangerous situations, their adventuresome spirit, and their dedication to improving the lives of others. They embody a diverse selection of ethnic, cultural, and geographic backgrounds. These narratives symbolize the myriad of women who sought new frontiers for countless reasons. More histories are waiting to be told—stories gathered from diaries, journals, and tear-stained letters left behind by these pioneering heroines. From this handful of histories, we can understand a great deal about the women who made history along the Arizona frontier.

By the mid-1800s, more than 250,000 people had crossed the continental United States heading west. They came with an assortment of desires, wishes, and resolves, seeking land, wealth, and freedom. Women often came with husbands, fathers, and brothers, and a few crossed the country of their own volition. Most began westward journeys in towns along the Missouri River, "jumping off places" where they loaded wagons with supplies before heading across the Great Plains of Middle America.

Wagon trains usually started out in late spring or early summer. Traveling in small cloth-covered carriages that only made about fifteen miles a day, pioneers believed they would reach their destinations within a few months. The majority of these caravans stayed on the road much longer. With few trails to follow, scant food supplies along the way, raiding Indians, floodwaters, and mountains to conquer, the way west often took as long as six to eight months.

Domestic chores occupied much of a woman's day on the trail, although women also drove wagons and livestock. They collected "buffalo chips" and weeds to fuel fires for meals often cooked over a handful of hot rocks. They watched over children and learned to keep an eye out for rattlesnakes, coyotes, buffalo, and bear. If they were lucky enough to find water, they washed the family laundry along the banks of sometimes-fetid streams. They tended the sick and injured, and buried the dead. And they gave birth under some of the most difficult conditions and circumstances.

Women came with anxiety and trepidation, fearing the unknown and yearning for those left behind. Yet they also traveled the road west with an eye toward the future. They marveled over the changing countryside, willingly tasted new beans and berries, and experimented with unknown vegetation. They relied on the close companionship of other women who were experiencing the same unique and unfamiliar adventures.

Arriving at their destinations, women set up housekeeping under extremely harsh conditions. Neighbors might be miles away and the men gone from home for weeks or months. Childbirth was often a lonely ordeal. They herded the animals, plowed the land, and planted and harvested crops. They cared for children, saw to their education, and cured their ills. They cleaned, cooked, and sewed. At night, when fearful solitude overtook them, they listened for the howl of a coyote or the hoot of an owl. Or worse, the sound of unwanted footsteps under their windows.

The Civil War slowed the flow of immigrants westward but certainly did not stop the pursuit for a better life. After the war, travel became more tolerable as stagecoaches and trains ventured into the wildness beyond the Mississippi River. Trading posts, stage stops, and eventually train depots sometimes meant travelers could purchase food along the way. People now traveled with a semblance of comfort and style.

While the Indian experienced the intrusion of incoming settlers long before the end of the Civil War, the arrival of even more colonists after the conflict put enormous pressures on tribes as their lands were swallowed up by waves of pioneers tilling the soil and growing unfamiliar crops. Native tribes were warned to stay off land they had roamed and cultivated for centuries.

Popular history records few narratives detailing the lives of Native American women coping with these new settlers who burned their homes and crops, destroyed their villages, and murdered their families. A handful of these women left histories of their plight and the search continues for additional stories so that a representative accounting of Native American women's history eventually will come to light.

WOMEN OF THE LAND

Land! Good land, rich land, free land. Land drove pioneers westward—the promise of fertile soil to grow crops, raise families, build homes, and start towns. The lure of gold and silver brought many into Arizona Territory, but it was the abundance of land that kept them here. Land meant prosperity, community, and continuity to uprooted pioneers.

Some traveled through the territory before settling here, as did Mary Aguirre, who journeyed with her husband up and down the 1,300-mile Santa Fe Trail from Missouri to Mexico, delivering supplies to army posts across the Southwest. The journal she composed during her travels portrays a lively young woman with an intense curiosity about the strange new lands she encountered as she made her way west.

Not all were happy with the circumstances that brought them into the territory. Ada Bass never adapted to the crude living conditions she endured on the rim of the Grand Canyon and often expressed her desire to return east, but she remained an integral part of one of the first tourist businesses at the canyon. And while Mormon Emma Lee French never expressed dissatisfaction with her lot in life, she survived untold hardships as one of nineteen wives in a polygamous family, living a lonely existence hundreds of miles from the nearest town at the site of what is now Lees Ferry.

The lust for land brought devastation to native peoples as pioneers encroached on their terrain, claiming it as their own. Indigenous tribes watched Anglo interlopers trample the unspoiled landscape with thousands of head of livestock, making little effort to understand native customs and beliefs. Disaster was imminent.

APACHE WARRIOR

Lozen

[CIRCA 1840–1889]

I saw a magnificent woman on a beautiful black horse—Lozen, sister of Victorio. Lozen, the woman warrior! High above her head she held her rifle. There was a glitter as her right foot lifted and struck the shoulder of her horse. He reared, then plunged into the torrent. She turned his head upstream, and he began swimming."

James Kaywaykla was a young Apache boy when he first saw Lozen ride into the swollen river. Throughout his life, he remembered the stalwart woman who fought beside her brother Chief Victorio, leader of the Chihenne band of Chiricahua Apaches. Kaywaykla's descriptions of Lozen's actions of bravery, her wisdom as a scout, and her accomplishments as a medicine woman may be the only firsthand accounts of her life.

Government interpreter John C. Cremony described an Apache woman who resembled the venerable Lozen in his 1868 book, *Life among the Apaches*. "There was one who received particular honor from the other sex, but her name has escaped my memory. She was renowned as one of the dexterous horse thieves and horse breakers in the tribe, and seldom permitted an expedition to go on a raid without her presence. The translation of her Apache title was 'Dexterous Horse Thief.'"

Historians place Lozen's birth sometime between the mid-1830s and 1840s, a time of intense hostilities between Apaches and white settlers. She probably grew up in southern New Mexico in an area known as Warm Springs, or Ojo Caliente, her childhood filled with the normal activities of all Apache children. But Lozen's athletic abilities outshone those of even the most gifted and agile boys. She learned early how to mount a horse without a bridle and could outshoot and outrun most of her peers.

As she matured, she acquired an adept knowledge of herbs and plants and was often called upon to minister to the injured and sick. According to James Kaywaykla, when Victorio was shot during a raid it was Lozen who cared for him. "She is skillful in dressing wounds," Victorio said. "When I got a bullet through my shoulder she burned the thorns from a leaf of a *nopal* [prickly pear cactus], split it, and bound the fleshy side to the wound. The next day I rode."

The ability to heal, along with an uncanny knowledge to detect enemies from great distances, were powers supposedly given to Lozen by Usen, the Apache Creator of Life. With outstretched arms, palms up, she turned to follow the sun. When she felt a tingling in her hands, and her palms darkened, she knew from which direction the enemy would come. Victorio relied upon Lozen's power. "Lozen is as my right hand," he said, "strong as a man, braver than most, and cunning in strategy. Lozen is a shield to her people."

Because of her skills and mystical talents, she sat beside Victorio at council meetings and participated in warrior ceremonies. Few Apache women reached the status Lozen experienced.

By the early 1860s, hostilities between incoming Europeans and the Apaches went beyond any chance of peaceful settlement. Victorio and Lozen, along with Nana, a respected Apache warrior (and Kaywaykla's grandfather), ransacked encroaching settlements in retaliation for the injustices inflicted upon their people. Yet by 1870, the military forced the Chihenne people from their land, moving them north to Tularosa, where New Mexico's fierce winds continually blew and crops failed to grow in the rocky soil. Four years later they were allowed to return to their home in Warm Springs, but within two years they were exiled once again, this time onto the San Carlos Reservation, a desolate spot in the harsh Arizona desert.

Victorio and his people bristled under the strict reservation rules imposed on them. In September 1877 three hundred Chihenne Apaches escaped from San Carlos, returning to their homeland in Warm Springs. Lozen led the women and children as the party left San Carlos. This may be when the young Kaywaykla saw her ride into the turbulent waters. The women faithfully followed the female warrior and watched fearfully as she rescued one horse and rider who drifted aimlessly downstream.

Two years later, they were once again ousted from Warm Springs and sent to New Mexico's Mescalero Reservation. When rumors circulated that Victorio was targeted for arrest, his band, including Lozen, fled to wander the Southwest, seeking shelter and provisions wherever possible.

Battles with the military took a devastating toll. During one skirmish, Victorio was shot in the leg. When soldiers ordered the Apaches to surrender, one woman shouted back that if Victorio were to die from his wound, they would eat him before turning him over to the soldiers.

Ammunition ran low for the struggling Apaches as they trekked across the desert. Lozen agreed to make the long arduous trip back to the Mescalero Reservation and return with more ammunition as well as additional warriors. Since she always felt it her duty to protect the women and children of the tribe,

LOZEN

she agreed to take with her a young pregnant woman who wanted to return to the reservation.

Shortly after departing, the woman silently gave birth in a secluded spot as Lozen watched soldiers pass by. During a birth, a female shaman such as Lozen usually sang and performed ceremonies to assure the health of mother and infant. With soldiers lurking everywhere, silence was a necessity and there was no time for such rituals. As soon as mother and child could travel, the trio headed out, carrying only a three-day supply of food.

As the women hid along the Rio Grande, Lozen saw an opportunity to add to their meager food supply. She watched as a herd of cattle entered the riverbed and lowered their heads to drink. With only a knife she killed one of the cows, a feat even a strong man would hesitate to undertake. But the meat gave the two women a few days' reprieve.

Water became a bigger issue, as they had no container to hold the precious liquid. To quench their thirst, they crushed moisture-laden nopal pads for whatever water they might hold.

With no horses, travel was dangerously slow. Lozen watched as Mexican soldiers came down to the riverbank to water their horses. As darkness approached, she hid mother and baby and swam across the Rio Grande, stealthily creeping into the soldiers' campsite. With a leather rope she had fashioned from the dead cow's hide, she slipped a lasso around the neck of one of the horses, leaped on, and fled just as the soldiers spotted her. Tearing down the riverbank, she raced to safety on the far bank, dodging bullets as she rode.

Days passed with little water. Lozen killed a calf and used its stomach for a makeshift canteen, but it held only a small supply of liquid. Detouring into Mexico to avoid U.S. troops, she stole another horse and eventually found a canteen on an unfortunate man who got in her way.

Finally arriving in Mescalero, Lozen learned that while she was transporting her precious cargo across the desert, Mexican troops had descended on Victorio. On October 14, 1880, Victorio and seventy-eight of his followers were slain at Tres Castillos. Sixty-eight were taken prisoner. Only seventeen escaped, including the elderly Nana.

Lozen hastened to join Nana and the few remaining forces. Revenge for Victorio's death consumed the small band. They rode across the land, killing whoever crossed their path. More than a thousand soldiers and civilians pursued the handful of Apaches, to no avail. They rode into Mexico and joined forces with the Chiricahua Apache Geronimo, who had also escaped from the misery of the San Carlos Reservation. The combined forces ravaged the countryside. "We were reckless of our lives," Geronimo later said, "because we felt every man's hand was against us."

During a battle with Mexican troops, the Apaches ran low on ammunition. According to one historian, Lozen spotted a pouch of cartridges that had been dropped inside the enemy fire line, and she crawled onto the battleground to retrieve the precious ammunition for her fellow warriors.

Within Geronimo's camp, Lozen met a young Chiricahua woman named Dahteste, who was fluent in English. As the friendship grew, Geronimo called on the two women to take messages back and forth to military personnel with whom he continually bartered for the surrender of his people.

Apache forces were disintegrating, their provisions depleted. Geronimo negotiated surrender with General George Crook, using Lozen and Dahteste to arrange the meeting. Nana agreed to return to San Carlos, but Geronimo refused. Lozen rode with Geronimo as he fled across Arizona Territory into the wilderness.

Times were changing, however. In 1886 Geronimo once again sent Lozen and Dahteste, with a message saying that he would agree to a meeting. By then, General Crook had been replaced by General Nelson A. Miles, who pursued Geronimo relentlessly until the warrior had no place to run.

In early September 1886 Geronimo surrendered. Lozen and Dahteste were with him, along with a handful of men, women, and children. Boarding a train in Bowie, Arizona, the entourage headed for an encampment in Fort Marion, Florida. The following year, the Apaches were relocated to Mt. Vernon Barracks north of Mobile, Alabama. Unused to the humid, swampy southern land, many died from a variety of illnesses, including diphtheria and tuberculosis.

Lozen lasted less than three years. On June 17, 1889, she died from tuberculosis and was buried in an unmarked grave. She never had a chance to return to her arid homeland and climb the tall mountains, face the sun, and listen once more for Usen to direct her power.

Dahteste survived bouts of tuberculosis and pneumonia while imprisoned in Alabama. She was eventually sent to a military prison in Fort Sill, Oklahoma, where she lived for the next nineteen years before being allowed to return to the Mescalero Apache Reservation. Many said she continued to mourn Lozen the rest of her life.

In 1913 the surviving Apaches were set free.

LEFT FOR DEAD

Larcena Ann Pennington Page Scott

[1837–1913]

In 1857 Elias Pennington brought his family of twelve motherless children into what was then New Mexico Territory (the area that became Arizona Territory a few years later in 1863), on his way from Texas to California, searching for more productive land. His wife Julia Ann had died two years before. Larcena Ann, born in Tennessee on June 10, 1837, was the third-oldest Pennington child.

About fifty miles east of Tucson, twenty-year-old Larcena took ill, probably with "mountain fever," or malaria. Rather than risk his daughter's health, Elias settled his family along Sonoita Creek until they could resume their westward journey. Before long a young lumberman, John Hempstead Page, came calling on the attractive Larcena. On December 24, 1859, they married in Tucson, supposedly the first Anglo couple to wed in the Old Pueblo, as Tucson has come to be called.

When John, who was employed by William Hudson Kirkland to fell trees and haul lumber, headed into the Santa Rita Mountains to chop down trees at a pinery, Larcena resolved to follow her new husband. She had not been feeling well and was advised that clean mountain air might cure her ills. For companionship while the men were away all day, she agreed to take ten-year-old Mercedes Sais Quiroz, a ward of Kirkland's, with her. Kirkland had asked Larcena to teach Mercedes the English language.

The morning of March 16, 1860 was brisk on the mountaintop, with patches of snow still clinging to the shadowed ridges. Nevertheless, the sun promised a bright clear day as Larcena hurriedly finished her chores around the Madera Canyon campsite. As Larcena told the story later, she still had to tutor Mercedes before she could rest, but sent the child outside to run off some of her youthful energy.

Bloodcurdling screams from the little girl sent Larcena tearing out of the tent. In front of Mercedes stood five imposing Tonto Apache warriors. As one of the Indians stood over the two women with his lance pointed at their throats, the other four looted the campsite's store of food and gathered as many goods as they could carry. They seemed particularly interested in John Page's clothing and took all his pants, shirts, and shoes. After destroying everything of no use to them, the five men motioned Larcena and Mercedes to move forward.

Their words meant nothing to Larcena, but Mercedes understood some of their Spanish dialect, recognizing enough words to conclude the Apaches were boasting to the women that they had killed John Page and his partner. Larcena could do little more than silently grieve for her husband.

As the women were force-marched deeper into the mountains, Larcena grew weaker as her chills and fever escalated. She and Mercedes snatched handfuls of snow to quench their thirst, their only source of sustenance.

Larcena tried to shield Mercedes from the constant jabs by the Apaches' lances and, without words, showed the child how to break off twigs and tear shreds of clothing to leave remnants along the trail on the chance someone would come looking for them. But believing her husband dead, Larcena had little faith anyone would discover their disappearance for days, maybe weeks.

Around sunset and about fifteen miles from the Page campsite, Larcena felt she could go no farther. Mercedes overheard the men talking about a search party coming their way. After much discussion, one of the men heaved Larcena over his shoulder and the group set off at an even faster pace.

The warrior only lasted a short while before throwing Larcena to the ground. Ordered to remove her heavy jacket, skirt, and shoes, the weakened woman meekly complied and turned to continue the arduous journey. In an instant, one of the Apaches grabbed his lance and jabbed it between her shoulders. The others joined the attack, repeatedly piercing her body. Pushing her down a steep ravine, they threw rocks at her inert body, convinced she would never survive. Only when she struck the trunk of a pine tree did she cease rolling toward certain death.

The Apaches left Larcena for dead and set off at an even faster pace with little Mercedes.

For three days she lay there, barely alive, waking only occasionally to searing pain coursing through her body, and the sound of her own screams of agony. She wavered between unconsciousness and an unending throbbing of her whole being. Patches of snow clinging to nooks and crevices, and the frozen earth beneath her battered body, staunched the flow of blood from the stab wounds, probably saving her from certain death.

During her days of delirium she thought she heard her husband's voice, but knew that could not be so. John was dead, killed by the same men who had left her on the mountaintop to meet the same fate. Yet she heard him again, and slowly realized that John really was calling her, that he was alive and looking for her. She tried to cry out, but her whimpers were barely audible. John passed by without knowing she lay in the ravine just below his footsteps.

LARCENA ANN PENNINGTON PAGE SCOTT

Two hours after Larcena and Mercedes were taken captive, John Page had returned to the disheveled and deserted campsite. Quickly assembling a posse, he headed into the mountains to rescue his bride. Twice he passed the ravine where Larcena lay, but he did not hear her feeble cries and continued to follow the prints of her shoes, now worn by one of the Apaches. Over the ensuing days more than fifty men came from Tucson and Tubac to join the search for Larcena and Mercedes.

Hearing the posse fade into the distance, Larcena knew she had to get off the mountain under her own power with whatever strength she had left in her shattered body. She struggled to her feet, clinging to the pine tree that had saved her life. Taking a few steps, she groaned in agony as inch by inch she maneuvered the steep incline. By the end of the day her feet were swollen and pitted with small pebbles, unable to support her. If she were to survive, she would have to crawl down the mountain.

Weak and half naked, she started her descent. Sometimes she crept downward but some days she had to go up the mountain before finding a pathway that would take her toward safety below. Her stab wounds bled profusely, weakening her even more.

She spied a bear's nest, a large matted heap of dried brush and grass, and was sorely tempted to crawl in and sleep. But fearing the bear would return, she moved on without comfort that night. If she found a sandy spot she dug a hole, covered herself with leaves and branches, and attempted to sleep for a while. However, with dawn's first light, as she tried to rise and continue her unbearable journey, she found herself so stiffened she had to wait until the sun warmed her haggard body before she could move forward.

Wild onions, seeds, and grass were her only nourishment until she spotted a rabbit grazing on grass she had expected to eat. Angry that the rabbit was dining on her supper, Larcena hurled a stone at the unsuspecting hare, killing it instantly. Only taking time to skin the poor creature, she later confessed, "No food ever tasted so good as that raw rabbit."

She came upon an abandoned campsite with a still-smoldering fire. Gathering up spilled coffee grounds and a handful of flour from the ground, she mixed the concoction with water from a nearby stream and baked her meager meal over the hot coals before devouring it by the fistful. That night she bathed in the stream and slept next to a warming fire.

Twelve excruciating days into her ordeal, Larcena spotted a wagon traveling along a road far below. Removing the remains of her tattered and blood-spattered petticoat, she shouted and waved the garment at the departing men, but her cries went unheard. Desperate and determined, she ran down the steep incline, disregarding her torn feet as she staggered and fell. But it took two days before she reached the base of the mountain where she had seen the wagon, and by then it was long gone.

She lurched and stumbled along the rutted wagon trail with little clothing left on her emaciated body. A man spotted this frightful apparition and almost ran in the opposite direction to escape the terrifying spirit that reeled toward him. Larcena, bloodied and bruised, her mud-clotted hair twisting and spiraling around her sunken face, clad only in a thin chemise that failed to cover her raw flesh, left the man doubting this was even a human being who appeared before him. But as she cried out he came to his senses, gathered her in, and carried her to a nearby lumber camp. Exactly two weeks had passed since the Apaches had invaded the campsite and taken off with the two women.

Doctors did not believe Larcena would survive, but she was not through with life yet. Although she bore the scars of her terrifying ordeal for years, she fully recovered.

A few days after Larcena's homecoming, little Mercedes Sais Quiroz was traded for a handful of Apache prisoners and returned home.

The following year, in March 1861, John Page was tortured and killed by a band of Apaches. Only his wallet, a handkerchief, and a lock of his hair were returned to his young widow. That September, Larcena gave birth to her first child, Mary Ann Page.

In 1871 Larcena married William F. Scott, after which she had four more children, and watched the town of Tucson grow into a bustling metropolis. Larcena Pennington Page Scott died on March 13, 1913, at the age of seventy-six. Pennington Street in downtown Tucson is not named for the resolute and determined Larcena, but rather for her father, Elias Pennington, who brought his family into southern Arizona intending to stay only a short while before moving on. Most of the Penningtons never left.

THE ROAD WEST

Mary Bier Bernard Aguirre

[1844–1906]

Curly haired Mary Bier Bernard probably had no idea what was in store for her when she married Epifanio Aguirre that steamy August day in 1862, but the world she had known for the previous eighteen years was about to change abruptly and dramatically. Born on June 23, 1844, in St. Louis, Missouri, Mary was a seasoned traveler to eastern metropolises and had acquired an excellent education that would serve her well. But her marriage to Mexican-born Epifanio would take her down western trails beyond her imagination.

Living in Westport, Missouri, a slave state at the outbreak of the Civil War, Mary was a devout Southerner, so much so that she helped sew the first two Confederate flags that Westport's soldiers took to war. Yet even as her family supported Southern troops, when Union soldiers marched into town, Mary's father Joab swore his allegiance to the North, to protect his wife and children.

Joab Bernard and Epifanio Aguirre had been conducting business together for years, and Joab knew Epifanio to be a fair and honest man. Epifanio drove mule and oxen trains along the Santa Fe Trail, delivering supplies to army posts throughout the Southwest. He and his men, sometimes numbering as many as three hundred, brought wagonloads of materials up from Chihuahua, Mexico, to Westport Landing, one of the largest trading centers on the Missouri River. His wealthy family had extensive holdings in both Mexico and New Mexico Territory. As the eldest son, he ran his family's vast empire. In 1860 he attended the Conference of National Government, held in Tucson, to petition Congress to create a separate territory, named Arizona, from the bottom third of existing New Mexico Territory.

Joab's Southern sympathies were well known throughout the region. His concern for his family's safety led him to offer Epifanio any amount of money to protect the Bernard family during this time of turmoil and strife among the states. Epifanio refused to take any money from his friend. What he wanted, he told Joab, was his daughter's hand in marriage.

It did not take eighteen-year-old Mary long to recognize the strength, kindness, and fairness of Epifanio. On August 21, 1862, she and twenty-nine-year-old Epifanio married in Westport.

By March of the following year, Epifanio prepared to return to Mexico for another shipment of goods. Skirmishes between Northern and Southern troops were rampant along the Missouri–Kansas border, making movement through the region extremely dangerous. He dared not take Mary with him, particularly since she was expecting their first child. Pedro Aguirre was born on June 26. Epifanio returned to Westport that August with a load of wool from Altar, Sonora, and by September, he was ready to get his wagons back on the road. This time Mary refused to be left behind.

Epifanio's routes were arduous and extremely dangerous. Mary had enjoyed her travels as a child, yet the journeys she took with Epifanio along the Santa Fe Trail were unlike anything she had previously experienced.

On September 19, the couple, along with three-month-old Pedro, left Westport for Las Cruces, New Mexico, where Epifanio's parents lived. Epifanio was hauling ten thousand pounds of freight in ten wagons with ten mules each. Along with his regular crew and a small guard to protect his precious cargo, Mary's father Joab, her sister Margaret, and a maid accompanied the Aguirres.

Mary thoroughly enjoyed the 1,300-mile adventure and found her accommodations in the large wagon, or ambulance, "marvels of comfort." Her traveling home resembled "a rather long carriage and the doors opened on the sides and had windows in them like hacks." She relished the pockets in the doors where she could store combs, brushes, and a looking glass. The mess (food) chest she considered as elegant as "a lady's china closet."

"I was like a child," she later wrote, "with no more knowledge of the responsibilities of life or the care of a baby and only glad to leave that cruel war and its horrors behind."

The wagons arrived in Las Cruces the week before Christmas, three months after leaving Westport. Don Pedro Aguirre and Doña Maria de Refugio Aguirre were delighted to meet their new daughter-in-law and grandson. By March Epifanio was again on the road, leaving Mary and Pedro at his parents' hacienda.

Through the years, Mary made three trips along the Santa Fe Trail, each one more difficult and uneasy than the last. She bore two more children: Epifanio Jr., born in Las Cruces on May 12, 1865, and Stephen, who arrived February 4, 1867, while the family was back in Westport.

The year 1869 began disastrously. Two of Epifanio's supply trains were destroyed—one in an Indian raid and the other by fire. With his business in ruins and his government contracts to haul army supplies cancelled, he had no choice but to move his family from Las Cruces to Altar, Sonora, where he and his brothers owned several companies that would keep them afloat.

Toward the end of July, the Aguirres set out from Las Cruces for Tucson before heading south into Altar, carrying a supply of wheat for the military. With a contingent

MARY BIER BERNARD AGUIRRE

of soldiers from Fort Bowie to protect them from Apache raiders, they maneuvered through Apache Pass, listening to the soldiers' stories of past Indian attacks. At one point they passed an overturned buckboard with hundreds of pieces of mail and newspapers scattered across the desert, the remains of a recent fateful encounter.

They arrived at Fort Bowie unscathed, and a second escort took them on to Tucson. Along the way Mary spotted fresh Indian tracks at almost every waterhole.

Safely arriving in Tucson, the party stayed put until August before venturing on to Altar, where they settled into a less elaborate lifestyle than that in New Mexico.

One of the family business ventures was operating a stagecoach that made regular trips to Tucson. On January 16, 1870, when the driver failed to show up, Epifanio took the reins of the stage and headed out of Altar for Tucson. As he approached a rest stop near Sasabe Flats, a barrage of bullets thudded into his body from several directions. According to the January 29, 1870 *Weekly Arizonian,* the men were attacked "by a large body of Indians... The Indians were concealed by the roadside, within the distance of half a mile from the station, and as the stage drove up fired into it, killing the driver [Epifanio] and another man, both of whom fell from the stage as soon as shot."

For five months Mary waited in Altar for her grief to pass, then took her three sons back to Westport. With no money of her own, she had few choices regarding how to provide for her children. Still an attractive woman, she could marry for convenience if she wished, or she could live with relatives who would help raise her boys. Neither option appealed to her.

In 1875 Arizona desperately needed schoolteachers. With Indian raids, bandits, and random killings still an almost daily occurrence, few dared venture into the territory. Yet Mary decided to return to the desert to teach.

Her first assignment placed her in the tiny community of Tres Álamos, just north of present-day Benson. Taking eight-year-old Stephen with her, she left the two older boys in Tucson in the care of Epifanio's brother Pedro, determining they needed the hand of a man to contain their youthful exuberance.

At Tres Álamos she roomed with a local family, the Dunbars, who ran a post office and stage station. With no door between the two bedrooms in the Dunbar house, Mr. Dunbar placed a blanket over the entryway for privacy. When the house filled with additional guests and more blankets were needed, Mr. Dunbar would ask Mary if he could "borrow the door" for the evening.

The little adobe schoolhouse contained no desks, chairs, or blackboard, and Mary had few school supplies for her twenty-three students. With Mr. Dunbar's help, she rounded up boxes for desks while the children sat on the floor.

The students progressed well under her tutelage until a balmy morning in April 1876 when an Apache warrior walked into the classroom. Uttering "good morning" to Mary and the students, the man sat down and began looking through one of the textbooks. Mary calmed the children and continued the class until the Apache finally rose and walked out of the schoolhouse.

Within the week, a nearby Indian raid claimed the lives of an entire family. Many believed the schoolhouse Apache had been closely watching the community. With her students fearful of leaving home, Mary and Stephen returned to Tucson. She was not without work for long.

When a teacher at the Tucson Public School for Girls took ill just a month before the term ended, Mary was asked to fill in. According to Mary, the twenty girls in the classroom "were the most unruly set of girls the Lord ever let live. They had an idea they conferred a favor upon the school and teacher by attending."

At recess time, the girls climbed out of the windows, freely romping through the streets of Tucson. Mary allowed this disobedient behavior one time before she refused to let the girls out of the schoolhouse. The next day, unhappy with their new schoolmarm, several students failed to appear, but those who did arrive behaved well. By the end of the week, however, under Mary's strict rules, only five girls remained in the class.

Fearing she would never be asked to teach again, Mary told her friend, territorial Governor Anson P. K. Safford, that she had "broken up your girls' school trying to keep order." Safford laughingly told his new teacher she should continue her discipline with his blessing.

The next week, all the girls were back in their seats and behaved admirably the rest of the term. Mary continued to teach at the school for the next three years, with enrollment in her classes steadily increasing. In 1878 she took ill and reluctantly resigned. That August she received another blow when thirteen-year-old Epifanio Jr. was struck by lightning and died.

The following year, her husband's brother Pedro, now ranching in Arivaca, built a school for the local children and asked Mary to become the community's first educator. Over the next decade, Mary taught her pupils and tended to the needs of her two surviving sons, as well as those of her elderly mother Arabella, who had moved to Arizona after Joab's death.

Mary's exemplary work in Arizona's rural schools caught the attention of officials at the University of Arizona. In 1896 she was asked to take the position as the first head of the university's Spanish language department. The *Tucson Daily Citizen* reported, "Mrs. Aguirre is a lady of exceptional talent, and educated both in Spanish and English to a degree which is a perfect guarantee of the excellent service she will render." The faculty and students knew the petite teacher as "the cheerful little professor with ringlets."

DOÑA EULALIA ELÍAS GONZÁLEZ

[1788~1865]

Doña Eulalia Elías González was born in the northern Sonoran town of Arizpe, Mexico. The González family controlled a vast ranching empire in what eventually became southern Arizona, with Doña Eulalia responsible for the financial well-being of their holdings. She possessed a tenacity well known among the Elías women, riding horseback alongside her brother Don Ignacio Elías González as they oversaw the flowing streams, verdant pastures, and abundant cottonwood trees of their San Ignacio del Babocomari land grant.

In 1832 Mexico granted Eulalia and Ignacio 130,000 acres along Babocomari Creek. For two decades she and another brother, Juan, handled finances for their thirty-mile-wide valley holdings between Sonoita Creek and the San Pedro River.

Energetic, proud, and sometimes difficult to deal with (according to her brothers), Eulalia ran the Elías properties with an astute mind and a firm hand. She visited Babacomari several times to assess the progress of their walled hacienda fortress and booming livestock business.

By 1840, forty thousand head of Elías cattle grazed along the Babocomari. By this time, however, Apache raids had driven many landowners back into Mexico. As one historian noted, these ranches were "little more than adobe islands in a desert sea—isolated, vulnerable, easily destroyed."

In 1849, after Apaches had killed two Elías brothers, the family abandoned their holdings and fled back to Arizpe. The remains of the Elías empire became part of the United States with the Gadsden Purchase in 1854. The irascible and still untamed Eulalia died in Arizpe on August 6, 1865.

While working for the university, she involved herself in the growth of the Tucson community. When the Society of Arizona Pioneers, established in 1884, refused to admit female members, Mary lobbied for the creation of the Ladies' Auxiliary of the Arizona Pioneers, which was finally recognized in 1902. Her friend and neighbor Larcena Pennington Page Scott became the auxiliary's first president and Mary served as the first vice president.

She also became an authority on Native American basketry and proudly presented a showcase of Indian baskets at the 1904 World's Fair in St. Louis, Missouri.

With her son Pedro happily ranching in southern Arizona, Mary spent her summers in San Francisco with son Stephen and his family. Train travel made the journey so much easier than those long-ago days when she knocked about in the bed of an ambulance along the Santa Fe Trail. She was quite content with her life as she boarded the Southern Pacific train for the coast on May 9, 1906.

Near San Juan, California, the train abruptly jumped the tracks, tumbling passengers into a pile of broken bones. Mary recounted the ordeal as just being "shaken up," but she lost the use of her right arm. Eventually, doctors determined she had sustained life-threatening internal injuries. On May 24, sixty-one-year-old Mary Bier Bernard Aguirre died from complications of the train wreck. When the *Tucson Daily Citizen* reported her death, they proclaimed, "No woman in the Southwest was better known than Mrs. Aguirre. She was a recognized authority on the history of New Mexico, Arizona, and Sonora."

LONESOME WOMAN
AT LONELY DELL

Emma Louise Batchelor Lee French
[1836–1897]

On May 25, 1856, the ship *Horizon* sailed out of Liverpool, England, for the United States. On board were 856 passengers recruited by the Church of Jesus Christ of Latter-day Saints, including twenty-one-year-old Emma Louise Batchelor, who had converted to Mormonism before leaving her Uckfield, Sussex County, home. By July 8, she was in Iowa City, Iowa, ready to start the long trek to Salt Lake City, Utah. The Church provided each traveler with a handcart to carry his or her belongings on the 1,400-mile walk. In return, each member would owe the Church one year of labor.

An educated woman, Emma must have known the risks involved in such a hazardous journey, but she cheerfully set out on foot with the Willie Company as it departed Iowa City.

By the time the travelers arrived in Fort Laramie, Wyoming, many of the handcarts were in disrepair. The company captain ordered everyone to remove most of their belongings to lighten their loads, but Emma refused to part with her meager possessions and stayed at Fort Laramie to await the Martin Company that was about ten days behind.

Before the Martin contingent could leave Fort Laramie, Emma was called on to serve as midwife, a role she would perform throughout her life. She later noted that once they were on the road, she carried the mother and newborn baby in her handcart for two days.

As the weather turned cold and bitter, the travelers struggled against unrelenting elements. Early snows in the Rocky Mountains left them sometimes stranded and often without food. Frostbite took its toll. More than 150 never made it to the land of Zion.

"I had no one to care for me or look out for me," Emma later told Mormon leader Brigham Young, "so I decided that I must look out for myself." At each stream, she shed her shoes and socks before wading into the freezing water. Once across, she briskly rubbed her feet with a woolen scarf to prevent frostbite. Unlike others who had no dry coverings for their feet, Emma survived the ordeal unscathed.

Owing the Church a year's service for surviving the march to Salt Lake City, Emma worked for Brother Kippen and his wife. Brother Kippen anticipated Emma would become one of his many wives, as the Mormons practiced polygamy until 1889. But Emma had other ideas and left as soon as her obligatory duty was fulfilled.

On December 27, 1857, she heard Brother John D. Lee speak at a meeting. She said she was captivated by his intelligence and good looks, and apparently he was just as delighted with the fair-haired young woman who stared at him for the duration of his speech. The two married less than two weeks later. On January 7, 1858, Brigham Young presided over the ceremony uniting John D. Lee and Emma Louise Batchelor. Emma was John's seventeenth wife.

The couple settled in New Harmony, Utah, where Emma cooked for John's extended family, including seven of his wives and their children. She bore five children here, and was busily content for the next several years. But factions were afoot that would tear down the structure of the Lee family's comfortable arrangement.

Several years before, Brigham Young had imposed martial law against all who entered Utah Territory. On September 11, 1857, emigrants traveling from

Arkansas to California were confronted by a band of Mormon men, along with a contingent of Paiutes, as they camped in Utah's Mountain Meadows valley. Informing the Arkansas contingent of Young's ruling, the Mormons offered to escort the wagon train back to Cedar City, Iowa. Then, without warning, they attacked the Arkansas families, killing 120 men, women, and children in one of the worst massacres in American history. John D. Lee was accused of participating in the bloodbath.

In May 1859 John heard soldiers were chasing down those involved in the Mountain Meadows Massacre, and he fled Harmony Valley. Heavily pregnant, Emma was unable to provide him with food and comfort while he hid out in the mountains. Instead, she expressed her concern for his safety in letters that were delivered by his other wives. "May God speedily permit you to return home," she wrote, "for I feel as though I could not stay from you much longer. I am sometimes tempted to try to climb the mountains in search of you." John returned to Emma's house shortly before she gave birth to their stillborn son.

For the next decade, the multiple Lee families lived in harmony. Emma never believed the stories of John's involvement in the Mountain Meadows Massacre, but John's past was about to catch up with him.

On October 8, 1870, the Mormon Church excommunicated John Lee for his actions in the Mountain Meadows Massacre. However, the Church also made it possible for him to live in relative secrecy and safety along the banks of the Colorado River on the border between the Utah and Arizona territories. His mission was to build a ferryboat and establish a crossing for Utah immigrants to reach Arizona and set up Mormon settlements. He took Emma and their children with him, arriving just before Christmas 1870. Emma surveyed her new surroundings and immediately named the place Lonely Dell, as it was the most desolate place she had ever seen. Years later, the site was renamed Lees Ferry.

Three weeks after their arrival, Emma and John had established a home fashioned out of rock. The two-room dwelling boasted a fireplace in each room to keep them warm during the winter months, while flagstone floors cooled the house during hot, sweltering summers. The following year, Emma gave birth to Fanny Dell, named after the loneliest spot in the world.

John was often gone for long periods, leaving Emma to handle the ferryboat as well as tend to household chores and the children. Travelers came and went by Lonely Dell, with Emma feeding most of them. Her reputation as a gracious and excellent cook soon spread.

In August 1872 Grand Canyon explorer John Wesley Powell visited Lonely Dell. Emma prepared such a delicious meal for his men that Powell mentioned the stopover in his journal. Before leaving, he gave her 150 pounds of flour and other groceries, more precious than any amount of money.

EMMA LOUISE BATCHELOR LEE FRENCH

Emma raised vegetables and tried to grow fruit trees along the Colorado River, but sudden turns in the weather often destroyed her crops. Storms blew in without warning, uprooting newly planted trees and flooding her gardens. Winds played havoc with the boats. In June 1873 a fierce gale loosened the ropes of the ferryboat, sending it downriver where it smashed against the shore.

About this same time, word reached Lonely Dell that a contingent of soldiers was headed toward the river. Fearing for his life once again John fled, leaving Emma to manage on her own. For three months she ran the ferry and tended the crops, house, and children. A flash flood destroyed much of the garden that summer, and the fruit trees burned in the blazing sun.

That August, a very pregnant Emma looked out her window to see a party of Navajos making camp just below her house. Still alone at the ferry and fearing the Navajos might break in during the night, she herded her children toward the Navajo encampment. She explained to the chief that they would be spending the night with them under the stars. When she awoke in the morning, the Navajos were gone. The chief later recalled the incident, describing Emma as a very brave woman.

As her due date approached with no sign of John, Emma realized she would have to give birth alone. Sending the children outside to play, she recruited her oldest son, Billy, to stay in the kitchen until she called him. After the baby girl was born, Billy helped cut the umbilical cord, then took the placenta outside and buried it. Emma rubbed parched flour on the little one's navel and slathered her with olive oil. She dubbed her newborn Victoria Elizabeth, in remembrance of her English homeland.

As 1874 blew in on a chilling gale, Brigham Young advised John Lee to title the ferryboat and land in Emma's name to protect the family. On November 7, 1874, John was arrested for the murder of 120 Arkansas souls and jailed in Beaver, Utah.

Anxious to get to her husband, Emma baked cookies and pies to take to John, along with a selection of books and some warm socks. As she entered the jailhouse, one of the guards asked another who she was. The reply sent Emma reeling as the second guard remarked she was one of John D. Lee's whores. He never saw her buggy whip until it sliced across his face.

Emma sent John what money she could spare for his defense, even as she fended off those who attempted to take the ferryboat and land from her. She was more than capable of running the crossing with the help of her older children and refused to allow anyone to threaten her livelihood and that of her family.

John's first trial ended with no decision, but a second jury found him guilty of murder in the first degree and sentenced him to die. On March 23, 1877, John D. Lee was taken to Mountain Meadows and executed.

Emma and the children struggled on at Lonely Dell for two more years. On May 16, 1879, at the insistence of the Mormon Church, she sold the boat and land back to the church for one hundred head of cattle, but she only received fourteen cows in payment.

Prospector and old friend Frank French agreed to travel with Emma and the children as they left Lonely Dell. As the days passed, an even deeper friendship formed between Emma and Frank. On August 9, 1879, the couple married in the town of Snowflake.

The following summer, Emma and Frank moved to the White Mountains area, but in the aftermath of the 1881 Battle of Cibecue, their house burned to the ground. Relocating to Holbrook, the couple opened a hotel. Emma cooked and tended to the needs of her guests, supplementing their meager income by selling her scrumptious baked goods around town.

When the railroad began work on a depot at Hardy's Station near Winslow, Emma opened another restaurant to serve railroad workers, travelers, and local folks. She and Frank moved to Winslow in the spring of 1887.

Through the years, Emma learned how to handle just about any medical emergency and knew the curative properties of numerous plants and herbs. Having served as midwife for some of John's wives and, of course, having delivered her own child, she was often called upon to care for the expectant wives of railroad workers. She set up a room in her house where women could come before they were due to give birth and where they could stay afterward as long as they wished. If an expectant mother could not get to Emma's "hospital," the railroad supplied an engine and car to take "Doctor French" wherever she was needed.

She was on call to the railroad, treating a variety of ailments and injuries that befell workers, as well as tending to the ills of the townspeople. One unproven story tells of Emma patching up a couple of drunken cowboys after the "real" doctor pronounced them both fatally wounded. When the diphtheria epidemic of 1891 hit Winslow, Emma spent long hours tending to patients, as well as her own children, all of whom came down with the disease.

While Emma was busy with her doctoring, Frank spent his time looking for silver along the Paria River. He was gone for long stretches, and in 1897 he disappeared for about six months. When he returned on November 13, Emma was delighted to see him and scurried into the kitchen to prepare her husband a meal. Without warning, she collapsed and died three days later.

Just about everyone in Winslow turned out to pay their respects to "Doctor French." Newspapers lauded her devotion to her patients. "No matter how inclement the weather, or what the hour of the day or night, she was always ready to respond to the call of the afflicted, whether rich or poor."

Trains coming in and out of Winslow silenced their whistles in deference to the woman who had saved so many lives.

GRAND CANYON MATRIARCH

Ada Diefendorf Bass

[1867–1951]

When Ada Diefendorf decided to take a pleasure trip to the Grand Canyon in 1894, she had no idea the excursion would alter her life completely. Up until that fateful expedition, time had moved her along at the pace of any refined, well-mannered nineteenth-century woman. She was an avid student and received her teaching certificate at age sixteen. Training herself to play the violin, she also took piano and organ lessons, all the while living comfortably with her parents in East Worchester, New York. Born August 26, 1867, the tall, somber, twenty-six-year-old woman was already beyond the age at which most young ladies married when she headed west.

She might have felt a little wanderlust as she set off for Prescott in 1893 to visit an aunt who managed the Commercial Hotel there. By the following spring, she had immersed herself in Prescott society by offering music lessons to local students.

That August she paid $25, took the train to Williams, and boarded a stagecoach with five other travelers for a tour of the Grand Canyon. The stagecoach owner and guide, William W. Bass, regaled his customers with the history of the canyon, recited poetry, and played the violin, much to everyone's delight. His talents certainly impressed Ada.

The entourage arrived at Mr. Bass's camp near the rim of the canyon around sunset, and Ada noted in her diary that she saw the "great panorama just as the light of day was being shaded by the curtain of night."

The next morning, the tourists continued their journey into the Grand Canyon, but Ada had little to say in her diary about the trip. What seemed to fascinate her even more was her guide, Mr. Bass.

William W. Bass had been taking sightseers into and around the Grand Canyon since 1885, when he established his first tourist site, Bass Camp, about twenty-five miles from the South Rim. He built roads from Williams and Ash Fork to the canyon, and bought a four-horse stagecoach, which he claimed was once used by General Nelson A. Miles during his Indian campaigns, to transport customers in relative comfort. He also constructed more than fifty miles of trails throughout the canyon.

At the bottom of the canyon, William created another campsite, Shinumo Camp, for those who wished to explore beyond the towering canyon walls and enjoy a more temperate climate during the winter months, when the rim was usually frozen and covered with snow.

Ada's party rode down one of the trails carved out by William to Havasu Canyon. By the time the group returned to the rim, the modest spinster was smitten with William Bass.

Within five months, Ada had returned to her family in East Worchester, gathered her belongings, and headed back to Arizona Territory to marry William Bass. On the evening of January 6, 1895, Ada and William, twenty years her senior, were married at the Methodist parsonage in Williams. She noted the ceremony in her diary and added that the *shivaree* thrown for the newlyweds (a boisterous celebration usually given to newlyweds the first night of their marriage) nearly drove her crazy.

The diary Ada kept so meticulously encompassed the years she and William lived at the Grand Canyon and is a significant reflection on her daily life, the fears and sorrows she faced, and the joys and delights she savored. Her words illustrate her struggle, and sometimes resistance, to the life she had chosen in the far northern reaches of Arizona Territory.

She learned to cope with the elements and accept the dangers and drudgery of maintaining a home for her family as well as catering to tourists who arrived on her doorstep expecting food, shelter, guidance, and entertainment. As more tents sprang up at Bass Camp to accommodate the ever-increasing number of tourists, Ada cooked and cleaned, often with only her own thoughts to keep her company.

She discovered in the first year of marriage that her husband had a proclivity for drinking and disappearing for days, leaving her to manage the tourist business along with family matters. Entries in her diary indicate he sometimes treated her with disdain, and a few passages suggest he struck her if he had consumed too much liquor. Yet she remained with him. Whether it was William she could not leave, or the wonders of the Grand Canyon, Ada never said.

A week after their nuptials, a photographer hired William to take him to the canyon. Ada "thought it would be fine to go along with them and get a taste

ADA DIEFENDORF BASS

of camping outside." Along with a man to look after the horses, the foursome headed north. Although she had already made the trip once, this would be her introduction into caring for her husband's customers, providing for their needs wherever they camped.

Several hours into the trip, rain poured from the sky as the party approached the Caves at Cataract Creek—a name William had given this stopping-off point. Ada tried to stay dry in the wagon as the men, soaked to the bone, maneuvered the horses and carriage across the swollen torrent.

"It was beyond the strength of the horses to start the load," she wrote. "While the men were busy with the animals, I was more than busy trying to save the perishable food, flour, sugar from the ravages of the water that was now seeping into the box of the vehicle. The men were soaked to the waist, but I was still dry. Luckily there was a pile of lumber nearby, and by propping the wagon tongue & using the planks, I was able to walk over them to the opposite bank."

She soon realized her married life would be comprised of numerous trips back and forth between the Grand Canyon, Prescott, Ash Fork, and Williams, often spending the night in the Caves at Cataract Creek, picking up or dropping off passengers, collecting supplies for the campsites, and sleeping wherever she could find a dry, albeit sometimes hard and cold, pallet. She once remarked that she had slept or prepared a meal under every tree between Ash Fork and the canyon. In October of her first year of marriage, she wrote, "Back to Caves again (God) how many times."

The couple had no permanent home and money was always scarce. As early as April 1895 she found herself forced to sleep in the stagecoach. By that August, she was washing dishes to earn enough money for food and retiring to the coach for another sleepless evening.

She sewed for the women of Ash Fork and Williams, washed dishes, played the piano at dances, and sold some of her precious heirlooms. Her December 31, 1895, entry summed up the frustration, exhaustion and depredation of her first year living as the wife of a tourist guide. "Thus endeth this horrible year, can the next be worse?"

Those first years traipsing from one camp to another—cooking, cleaning, and catering to tourists—left Ada exhausted and discouraged. Her diary records endless days of "hunting horses and cleaning up dirt." She became so weary of repeating her own words that she started using the abbreviation "SOS" (same old story) instead of detailing her daily activities.

In March 1896 Ada was pregnant with her first child. She and William found themselves stranded at the Caves with few provisions and William quite ill. She melted snow for drinking water and sawed logs from the corral for firewood, although she had little food to cook over the meager flames. "I walked, in different directions from the camp each day, hoping to find a horse I could use to ride for help. I wrote notes and fastened them on bushes along the road telling of our plight and I hoped someone passing would find them."

For eight weeks, she tended to her ailing husband and rationed their scant food supply. Finally she found an old horse and brought it back to camp. It was thirty-five miles to Ash Fork, notwithstanding the weather, but she knew she had to go for help. Just as she was ready to leave, a stranger appeared on the horizon. Ada hailed him and implored him to go to Ash Fork for help. For two days, she paced the floor, praying the man made it through. At last, she heard a wagon outside her door and knew their lives had been spared.

That spring, Ada was forced to sell "my embroidered bed spread & sham & a fine pieced quilt & pillow slips with lace" to put food on the table. Two days later, she "sold Mrs. Broylis my silverware and music book to buy something to eat."

In May, she returned to her mother in East Worchester to give birth to her first child, Edith Jane, born August 20, 1896. She would not return to the Grand Canyon, and her husband, until Edith was three years old.

January 1900 was exceptionally cold as Ada rode down the canyon trail to Shinumo Camp. Beside her, three-and-a-half-year-old Edith excitedly viewed her amazing surroundings as she rode her horse into the abyss. Ada proudly boasted her young daughter was "probably the first child to ride a horse to the [Colorado] River alone."

But if Ada had known Edith would spend the rest of her life riding up and down these trails, toiling for the pleasure of her father's customers, she might have turned around and taken Edith right back to East Worchester. By the time she was ten years old, the youngster was herding horses and mules up and down the canyon, catering to the whims of sightseers. Edith Jane Bass became the Canyon's first female wrangler.

That winter, the family decided to stay at the bottom of the canyon, where temperatures were warmer than at the rim. Shinumo Camp benefited from an orchard replete with fig, peach, and apricot trees. The garden held a multihued variety of melons, beans, tomatoes, squash, and grapes. Although they lived in tents, William built a stone fireplace and table for their dining pleasure. A few tourists ventured into the canyon that winter, but for several months Ada happily looked after her young daughter without the drudgery of catering to strangers.

When they returned to the rim that March, Ada was pregnant with her second child. William Guy "Bill" Bass was born in Williams July 26, 1900. On young Bill's first trip into the canyon, Ada placed him in a sling on one side of a burro with the family dog on the other side to balance the load.

Ada reared four children at the canyon, staying with her husband despite his inability to hold onto a dollar, his drunken tirades, and occasional flings with other women. She is considered the first Anglo woman to rear a family on the rim of the Grand Canyon.

Her son Bill knew how much his mother endured. "Nearly thirty years of her life was spent caring and cooking for tourists. When no other guide was available she often escorted our guests to the river, and for months at a time stayed alone with us kids—seventy-three miles from the nearest town—while Dad would be off somewhere on business…"

She was responsible for planning and ordering food and supplies for all the campsites. Inventories and bookkeeping duties also fell on her shoulders. When she was unavailable, or away having babies, the entire operation slowed to the pace of a stubborn mule, and she often returned to an enormous mess of unordered supplies, unwashed clothes, and dirty dishes.

If the spring runoff or July storms did not produce a sufficient supply of water in the cisterns, Ada dutifully packed the family's dirty laundry on a mule and rode down the canyon to the Colorado River, spent the night, washed clothes the next day, and returned to the rim the following day. In 1904 she wrote, "I'm tired enough to die & can't stand this much longer & no one to help me."

Not until 1906, after she gave birth to her last child, did Ada finally realize a proper home for her family. Near Bass Camp, the couple built their first permanent home, called the White House, complete with warehouse, corrals, cistern, and storage facilities.

With a proper home, even though tourists still stayed overnight, Ada found a few years of peace. She tended her vegetable garden and home-schooled the children, since there were no educational facilities yet at the canyon. When they could afford it, she took the children to Phoenix to attend school.

With the arrival of train travel to the Grand Canyon in 1901, what used to be a two-day stage ride from Williams could now be accomplished with a swift three-hour, comfortable rail ride costing a mere $3.95.

The railroad also brought competition in the form of the Fred Harvey Company, which had reached an agreement with the Santa Fe Railroad to provide restaurants for its passengers. When the Grand Canyon became a national monument in 1908, visitors flocked to the South Rim.

By 1911, tourist traffic consisted mainly of day visitors instead of those who had previously stayed for longer periods. Since Fred Harvey's establishments provided nourishment and housing right at the rim of the canyon, the Basses' tourist traffic farther down the road declined.

In 1912 Ada and William established new quarters at the edge of the canyon.

With siding made of pressed tin, this home was aptly named the Tin House. Once again, Ada settled into her new surroundings and tried to establish a comfortable environment for her family.

But business again changed after the canyon was recognized as a national park in 1919 and the Fred Harvey Company was awarded the primary concession franchise on the South Rim. The Basses' days in the tourist business were numbered. On September 15, 1923, the couple said goodbye to their last paying guest.

In 1927 they sold all their holdings to the Santa Fe Railroad for $20,000. Ada insisted that half the proceeds be put in her name. She had been an integral part of their tourist business for more than thirty years, and she felt she had earned her share of the profits.

The couple moved to Wickenburg, where William died in 1933. Eventually Ada settled in Phoenix.

In her declining years, her son Bill took her back to the canyon for one last visit. "She sat on the porch at the lodge for a long time, watching the canyon, looking at things only her eyes saw. And then she spoke, as if answering a question that echoed across the years: 'I love the canyon, too,'" she whispered.

WOMEN WHO HEALED AND SAVED

Health care in the early Southwest relied mainly on military hospitals, if one was nearby. Otherwise, settlers were on their own, with women in particular responsible for the well-being of their families.

Diseases such as dysentery, smallpox, and syphilis were prevalent in most desert towns. Malaria and scurvy ran rampant through military posts. Malnutrition took many lives, especially in desert regions where refrigeration was nonexistent and food spoiled within hours. Injuries from arrows and bullets festered and became infected so quickly that death was often imminent regardless of how minor the wound.

Even if one was lucky enough to live near an army post, recovery was not guaranteed. An early description of the hospital at Camp Lowell in Tucson illustrates the primitive conditions that left many patients more dead than alive:

The Camp consists of two hospital tents, roughly fitted together, with tables and benches. The hospital is an old adobe building on the main street of the town, at a distance of about one thousand yards from the camp. Even if this building was in good condition, its position in the center of the town, its proximity to the irrigated fields in the river bottom, of its distance from camp, and the smallness of its rooms, render it undesirable as a hospital; but when, in addition to this, its leaky roof, worn out floor, and rain washed walls are taken into consideration, and the series of old sinks that are covered up in its enclosure, it is found to be totally unfitted for such a use.

Women have been responsible for the ill and injured since time began, yet for years they were precluded from medical training or licensing. When Elizabeth

Blackwell, the first woman to obtain a medical degree, applied to Geneva Medical College in New York in 1847, officials looked to the all-male student body to determine if she should be admitted. Thinking it a joke, the men voted her in.

Male physicians argued that women were too frail and delicate to view the intimacies of the human body and too emotional to handle the horrors of surgery, the scourge of disease, and the shame in examining a naked torso, even though they had been doing all these things without training or a license for centuries. Doctors thought women would lose their femininity, even their minds, if they became physicians, although they praised the backbreaking work nurses performed.

If women were considered incapable of earning the title "doctor," they could certainly save lives with their knowledge of curative plants and herbs derived from old European cultures. Theresa Ferrin brought numerous holistic practices and a comprehensive understanding of healing herbs and plants from her German homeland, earning her the title "Angel of Tucson" as she tended to the ills of the populace. And although Teresita Urrea's life history is a combination of fact and fiction, she was considered a saint for her hands-on healing powers and use of medicinal plants.

Florence Yount is recognized as the first woman physician in the Prescott area, devoting her practice mainly to obstetrics and pediatrics. When a new hospital lacked funds for a stove to keep patients warm, she hauled one into town from an old mining camp to ward off chills on cold winter nights.

Many who accepted the vows of chastity and charity also made their way west. Some came the hard way, as did the seven Sisters of St. Joseph of Carondelet, who trudged across the blazing desert enduring untold hardships, unwelcome marriage proposals, and the relentless sun to reach the distant village of Tucson. Those who came after them were afforded more comfortable travel by stagecoach and later by train. However they made it here, they were truly needed and celebrated by towns and cities as they established schools, hospitals, and missions. They brought medical aid, education, and solace to the most distant destinations. Many of them deserve to be recognized as saints, as was Katharine Drexel, who gave away her vast fortune to bring education and Christian principles to the Navajo Nation.

Very few women who tended to the medical and religious needs of the western populace were recognized for their work. Those who left footsteps to follow and lives to emulate must represent those who performed beyond the call of duty in silence, sometimes solitude, lest they disappear altogether.

FROM OUT OF THE DESERT

Sisters of St. Joseph of Carondelet

[1870–PRESENT]

For more than one hundred years, the Sisters of St. Joseph of Carondelet have tended to the educational and medical needs of the citizens of Arizona, particularly in Tucson. Their appearance in the territory was nothing short of miraculous as they marched into the Old Pueblo on the warm spring evening of May 25, 1870. Sister Monica Corrigan, one of the original seven nuns who journeyed from the Motherhouse in St. Louis, Missouri, to Tucson, chronicled their terrifying passage across the desert, braving dangers both two- and four-footed, tipsy rafts, and threats of Indian attacks. The other six courageous souls were sisters Ambrosia Arnichaud, Hyacinth Blanc, Emerentia Bounefoy, Martha Peters, Euphrasia Suchet, and Maximus Croisat, who described the vast wasteland that lay before her as "the abomination of desolation."

Their wagon out of San Diego was only big enough for six of the women. Sister Ambrosia rode beside the driver, enduring the ravages of sun and sand as they set out for Tucson.

Several days of blistering heat, along with cold, arid nights, brought the group to a ranch house where they were offered a hot meal. Since few of the cowboys around the table that evening had seen a woman in months, proposals of marriage flew through the air like a wild dust storm. "The simplicity and earnestness with which they spoke put indignation out of the question," wrote Sister Monica, "as it was evident they meant no insult, but our good."

Arriving at the Colorado River, the sisters boarded a raft to carry them into Arizona Territory. The overcrowded ferry dipped dangerously close to spilling everyone into the deep, murky waters.

Father Francisco met them on the other side for the final two-hundred-mile trek to Tucson. As the sisters walked most of the way, their heavy black habits took on a ghostly earthen hue as they swept the desert floor. At each break in their travels, they painfully removed thorny cactus needles embedded deep in their feet.

The weary entourage followed the Gila River, passing unmarked graves of those who had faltered along the way or who had encountered marauding Indians. "One of these [graves], we were informed, contained the remains of a father, mother and five children," Sister Monica noted. When the sisters stopped for a break one day, however, an assemblage of Indians approached the party. "Sister Martha was resting on an old cowhide. A noble warrior, perceiving her, stole softly up and sat down beside her as her guardian angel."

Two days out from Tucson, soldiers joined the party as an escort into Tucson. More soldiers arrived the following day as the sisters headed through a narrow corridor at Picacho Peak, a place known for Indian attacks.

" 'The Indians! The Indians!' was echoed from every mouth. Whips and spurs were given to the horses—we went like lightning—the men yelling like so many fiends, in order to frighten the savages. The novelty of the scene kept us from being afraid." Sister Monica seemed to enjoy the wild ride.

As the nuns entered Tucson, hundreds rejoiced at their safe arrival. "The city was illuminated, fireworks in full play," Sister Monica reported. "All the bells in the city were pealing forth their merriest strains." The first seven Sisters of St. Joseph of Carondelet had arrived, weary and footsore, but ready to go to work.

They had been asked to come and establish a school. A few scholarly institutions had been attempted in Tucson, but most failed for lack of funds. Within days of their arrival, the sisters opened St. Joseph's Convent and Academy for Females. According to Sister Monica, "We had scarcely time to brush the dust off our habits before opening school."

With the school always overcrowded, the sisters ventured into mining camps, begging for donations to keep the institution afloat. On one occasion, a miner handed one of the sisters a large sum of money representing several months' wages. It seemed the miner had appeared at the academy door on Christmas Day, drunker than a Saturday night cowboy. One of the sisters fed him a hearty meal accompanied by a stern sermon on the evils of liquor. Apparently, he appreciated both the food and the lecture.

An advertisement in the *Tucson Citizen* promised classes of "every useful and ornamental branch suitable for young ladies" at the academy. Elocution, physical geography, history, grammar, composition, botany, astronomy, and intellectual and practical arithmetic were only part of the agenda. "Particular attention paid to plain and ornamental needlework—free of charge," the ad guaranteed.

Within three years, the sisters were also operating a school at the San Xavier Mission for Tohono O'odham (formerly known as Papago) students. The year before Yuma Territorial Prison was completed in 1876, they went back to the muddy Colorado River and started Sacred Heart School. They established St. Theresa's School in Florence in 1877, St. Joseph's Hospital in Prescott in 1878 (later converted into a school), and St. John's vocational school at Komatke on the Pima reservation in 1901.

SISTERS OF ST. JOSEPH OF CARONDELET

Working in the outlying Indian schools presented more challenges, as Sister St. Barbara Reilly discovered. She came by train from the Motherhouse in 1881, having been diagnosed with tuberculosis. As so many before her, she hoped the dry southwestern air would cure her of the debilitating disease. When the train stopped at a wayside, a crusty old cowboy pulled up in a handcar on the adjoining track and asked where she was going. Discovering she was headed for Tucson, the man gave her a bag of fresh peaches and shouted as he pulled away, "Home with your mother you ought to be!" Sister St. Barbara enjoyed the peaches anyway.

Coming from the East, the novitiate was surprised to find that candlelight was the only means of illumination. Dirt floors had to be slopped down with water to keep the dust at bay. Yet Sister St. Barbara stayed in the Southwest for over forty years, teaching Yuma, Pima, and Tohono O'odham children as well as working in many of the missions.

The true Wild West greeted her in 1887 when she rode alone on a stagecoach from Prescott to Tucson. When the driver asked if she would hide a small box beneath her long dress, she thought nothing of it until an outlaw appeared out of nowhere and held up the stage. As soon as the bandit saw the imposing black habit of Sister St. Barbara, he turned tail and left. The stage driver was truly thankful for her cooperation as the box she protected held several thousand dollars.

In 1876 the sisters completed work on a new provincial house and novitiate in Tucson. Mother Irene Facemaz became the first superior of Mount St. Joseph Novitiate.

Twenty-seven-year-old Gabriella Martinez Otero, born in Tucson, walked through the doors of the adobe novitiate in 1877 to begin her training. Nearby ranch children flourished under Gabriella's tutelage while she waited to take her vows. In 1880 she chose the name Sister Clara of the Blessed Sacrament and entered the family of the Sisters of St. Joseph, moving into St. Joseph's Academy to teach classes in Spanish and art as well as piano, harp, guitar, and violin.

She was one of six Tucson women who took their vows at Mount St. Joseph shortly after its inception. Mary Agnes Orozco, Amelia Leon, and Teresa Ortiz were professed as sisters in 1879, while Mary Joseph Franco and Mary John Noli stood alongside Sister Clara in 1880.

The novitiate was converted into an orphanage in 1886, but the structure was only large enough to house about thirty children. In 1901 a violent windstorm damaged the orphanage beyond repair. Sister Angelica Byrne determined to rebuild the orphanage and set about collecting alms from mining camps, riding in cabooses of freight trains and walking miles to reach each encampment. She even followed the miners underground if it meant a few more dollars in the pot.

In four years Sister Angelica raised $16,000. Acquiring forty acres of land, the new St. Joseph's Orphanage opened in 1905 with room for one hundred children.

Of all the schools and missions the Sisters of St. Joseph founded and managed, their most significant contribution was the establishment of Tucson's St. Mary's Hospital, today a multistoried health care center that provides care, compassion, and comfort to thousands of patients.

Bishop J. B. Salpointe had initially asked the sisters to come to Tucson to teach; now he wanted them to run the hospital. Already providing medical aid by going house to house, the sisters opened the doors of St. Mary's Hospital on April 24, 1880. The diminutive stone and adobe structure consisted of one floor for patients and a basement occupied by a kitchen and dining room, laundry, and storage area. Mother Basil Morris ran the hospital, together with sisters Mary John Noli, Julia Ford, and St. Martin Dunn.

"There were only three doctors and two sisters besides myself working in the hospital," wrote Sister Mary John. "Sister St. Martin worked with the doctors and the books, and Sister Julia and I were in charge of the twelve bed ward. It was hard work." In addition to their nursing duties, the four women washed and ironed all the linen used at the hospital, scrubbed floors, cooked, and served meals to the patients. They produced some of the food in their own garden and dairy. One large wood stove heated water for patients' baths as well as sterilizing surgical instruments. Coal oil lamps and candles were the only light available at night.

"We usually arose at five in the morning," according to Sister Mary John, "but often as early as one if we were to get all our work done, and sometimes we did not sleep at all if there was a sick patient who could not be left alone."

In 1882 the sisters purchased the buildings and grounds of St. Mary's Hospital, which allowed them more freedom to implement their plans for the facility.

Mother Fidelia McMahon became head of St. Mary's in 1893. Under her leadership, the hospital grew and expanded far beyond its original minuscule start into a modern, full-service health center. She instituted a surgical area that included a sterilization room, operating room, emergency room, even a place to tie up ambulance horses. In 1900 Arizona's first sanatorium for tuberculosis patients was built adjacent to the hospital.

A cave on the hospital property provided the perfect spot to lay down pipes that brought refrigeration into the buildings. Ice blocks were placed above the pipes, providing cool, refreshing water for patients. Mother McMahon went into her own pocket to pay the first installment on a steam plant for the hospital.

In 1914 Sister Fidelia initiated St. Mary's School of Nursing to provide better care for hospital patients. The school gained accreditation in 1922.

"Now that we are settled in our new home," wrote Sister Monica in her last journal entry, "we trust our good sisters will continue to pray for us; recommending the success of our missions, our schools and our own spiritual welfare, to our dear Lord, to the end that we may labor earnestly to promote His greater glory, and have this, alone, in view, in all our undertakings." Her prayers were certainly answered, for out of the desert, seven courageous women, and those who followed, brought education and health care to the citizens of Arizona. The schools, missions, and hospitals they established are a legacy and testimony to their devotion and tenacity.

CURANDERA

Teresita Urrea
[1873–1906]

Teresita's childhood was anything but idyllic. The bastard child of a rich Mexican landowner and a fourteen-year-old Tehueco Indian servant, she was born into poverty in Ocoroni, Sinaloa, Mexico, on October 15, 1873. Her father, Don Tomás Urrea, was not aware of her existence. She lived with her mother Cayetana Chávez and an aunt, both of whom worked for Don Tomás. The little girl with auburn hair and soft brown eyes thrived under the Mexican sun, playing rough-and-tumble games and riding across the plains at hell-bent speed.

Her full name was Niña Garcia Nona Maria Rebecca Chávez, but the petite and lively spirit came to be known as Teresita.

She was born shortly before Mexico fell under the autocracy of Porfirio Díaz, who controlled the country's political arena for more than thirty years. Young Teresita found herself caught up in the turmoil and disorder that spread across the country under Díaz's sovereignty.

In 1876 General Díaz took the dictatorial reins as president of Mexico. When Don Tomás refused to support Díaz, he found himself under orders to round up his family, servants, and livestock and leave his Ocoroni homestead. Don Tomás settled most of his flock on his ranch in Cabora in the state of Sonora, but left some of his retainers to run his holdings in nearby Aquihuuiquichi, including young Teresita and her mother. Sometime during the next ten years, Cayetana abandoned her child.

Around 1888 Don Tomás became aware that the lively young adolescent who lived at Aquihuuiquichi was his daughter and sent for the fifteen-year-old to live with him at Cabora. Determined hands thrust her bare feet into fashionable shoes, and her lithesome body was pushed and prodded into tightly corseted gowns. Her hair was fashionably coifed and she could no longer ride across the plains and sing with the vaqueros. She had to learn to conduct herself like a wealthy landowner's daughter.

She spent much of her time with Huila, an elderly servant who had overseen the Urrea household for years. Huila was a *curandera*, or healer, serving the Indians in the area as well as the Urrea family. Teresita became interested in the herbs and plants Huila used to cure the ills and set the bones of those at the hacienda and in surrounding villages. Weeds, grass, tree roots, even cactus were all part of the old woman's medicine bag. Before long, Teresita could distinguish which plants would ease the pain of childbirth, cure a lingering illness, or calm a distressed patient.

Huila recognized in Teresita abilities far beyond her own skills. She witnessed the young girl ease the suffering of many a patient by holding a hand and gazing into the sufferer's eyes. As the curandera administered her potions, Teresita soothed away the agony and brought calmness to the bedside. The two women became a formidable team against the ills of both mind and body.

About a year after she entered the Urrea household, Teresita was stricken with an unexplainable cataleptic state that left her comatose. Speculation still surrounds the mysterious event that put the young woman into this catatonic trance, with many believing she was attacked by a man who tried to rape her. For almost two weeks she lay without movement, taking no food or water, her breathing barely discernible. The women of the household prepared for her wake and Don Tomás ordered the construction of her coffin.

As the family prayed over the inert body, the young girl suddenly sat up. She said she had spoken to the Virgin Mary, who explained she now possessed extraordinary powers and should use them to cure and comfort those in need.

She asked about the coffin that lay beside her and was told it had been built for her funeral. Teresita replied she would not require the coffin, but in three days it would be needed for someone else. When old Huila died during this three-day period, she was placed in the coffin meant for Teresita.

Over the ensuing months, Teresita frequently went into a trance but woke to administer her healing powers to those who came seeking her mystic gifts. Her reputation went beyond the local villages, and before long thousands came to the Urrea hacienda in search of the girl with the miracle cures. She administered the medicinal herbs and plants that Huila had taught her to use, and sometimes

TERESITA URREA

scooped up a handful of earth and mixed it with her own saliva to elicit a cure. Her compelling eyes held the patient in a trancelike state as she soothed the affected body with her healing hands. Her ministrations bewitched the local Indians. The Tomóchic hailed her as their patron saint. She became known as "La Santa de Cabora."

As word spread of Teresita's skills and talents, she attracted the attention of both the Catholic Church and President Porfirio Díaz. Proffering that the love of God and love for one's fellow man were all that was needed to eliminate war, poverty and injustice, she drew the wrath of the Church by suggesting the prayers of priests were not necessary, that one could pray directly to God. In 1891 the Church denounced her as a heretic.

The Yaqui Indians believed Teresita had been sent by God. President Díaz, however, considered her an instigator who was agitating the Indians against his government. He demonstrated his wrath by destroying the Tarahumara Indian village of Tomóchic and placing Teresita under surveillance. In 1892 he ordered her escorted out of Mexico. Don Tomás and Teresita crossed into the United States at Nogales that July, leaving behind the rest of the family and all their possessions.

Before long Díaz realized his mistake in letting the girl go. He now had no control over her influence among the Indian people. His request to U.S. authorities to return her to Mexico went unheeded.

With Indians still seeking Teresita's healing powers and Díaz threatening to take her back to Mexico, Don Tomás hastily took his daughter to Tucson to apply for U.S. citizenship. But Teresita was only nineteen, not yet old enough to become a citizen. Hoping to avoid additional confrontation with the Díaz government, father and daughter accepted an invitation to move to the eastern Arizona community of San José near the New Mexico border. They only stayed eight months before relocating to El Paso, Texas. Regardless of where she lived, the sick and injured followed her, begging for the touch of her hand and relief from their sorrows.

In El Paso, Teresita received several threats on her life, forcing Don Tomás to move once again farther from the border. They settled in Clifton, Arizona, in 1897.

In Clifton, Teresita found peace and solace. She was happy there, although it did not take long before local citizens came knocking on her door for relief from innumerable troubles. There were reports that she helped ease the suffering of a young Clifton boy stricken with polio.

As she had with Huila's death, Teresita sometimes predicted the future. She foresaw her own marriage, but also envisioned her husband would try to kill her.

In 1899 she fell in love with a local miner, Guadalupe Rodriguez, much to Don Tomás's angst. Defying her father, Teresita and Rodriguez married on June

22, 1900. The following day, Rodriguez ordered Teresita to prepare to return to Mexico. When she refused, he dragged her out of the house, pulling her along the railroad tracks. He rushed ahead of her and without warning turned back to Teresita, pulled his gun, and shot at his new wife, barely missing her. He was eventually caught, found insane, and sent to an asylum. Whatever Rodriguez's motives, Teresita and those around her presumed he was an agent of President Díaz sent to return her to Mexico. The marriage lasted all of one day.

Knowing she had hurt her father terribly by marrying against his wishes, Teresita left for California, hoping distance might heal the wounds between father and daughter. She never saw Don Tomás again.

While in California, she helped cure a young girl and the newspapers began exploiting the story of the "miracle worker." Another report claimed she alleviated the pain of a boy suffering from spinal meningitis even though five doctors had pronounced him incurable.

She attracted the attention of a medical company that offered to send her across the country to heal people free of charge. She would be paid $2,000 a year for her services.

Accepting the offer, Teresita quickly realized she was unable to communicate with non-Spanish-speaking patients in states north of the Mexican border. She asked a friend to send one of her sons to interpret for her. Nineteen-year-old John Van Order traveled with Teresita as her translator, and within a few months, word spread that Van Order and Teresita had married, even though her divorce from Rodriquez would not be final for three more years.

In 1902 the couple was living in New York when Teresita gave birth to their daughter Laura. That same year, Don Tomás died of typhoid fever without reconciling with Teresita. He was buried in the Clifton cemetery.

The couple eventually moved to Los Angeles, but when Teresita found herself pregnant again, she returned to Clifton, where her daughter Magdalena was born in 1904.

Back in Clifton, where she felt accepted and content, Teresita built a house from the proceeds of her tour money and settled in with her husband and two daughters. A local newspaper quoted her as planning "to nurse the sick to health and to heal the wounds of the injured" in her new house. All too soon, however, she was diagnosed with tuberculosis and given but a short time to live. Because she was contagious, doctors warned her against seeing patients. John Van Order was still a presence in Teresita's life, but seemed to have little cognizance of her needs during her illness.

As time ran out for Teresita, she held onto life with the premonition that her mother, whom she had not seen for almost thirty years, was coming. Cayetana

Chávez arrived just before Teresita died on January 11, 1906, at the age of thirty-three. More than four hundred people attended her funeral in Clifton. She is buried somewhere in the area, but her grave remains unmarked.

Teresita touched countless lives during the few years she was alive. She inspired people in need, healed those she could, and comforted the incurable. Many believed she was a saint; others acknowledged her healing abilities but scoffed at the notion she communicated with the Virgin Mary. Whatever her talents, she made a difference to a host of suffering souls during her short time on earth. Even today, she remains in the hearts and minds of contemporary Hispanics.

ANGEL OF TUCSON

Theresa Marx Ferrin

[1846–1911]

The Jewish community of old Tucson was cohesive and active in the late 1800s, even though it had no synagogue in which to pray. Through the efforts of a petite, energetic woman, Tucson Jews acquired their first place of worship and the first synagogue in Arizona Territory.

Born in Germany in 1846, Theresa Marx immigrated to San Francisco with her family around 1874. She was working as a milliner when she met Joseph Ferrin, a tailor from Tucson. The two married on June 23, 1878, in a San Francisco Russian-Polish synagogue and almost immediately boarded a train for Yuma, then headed by stagecoach for the Old Pueblo.

Joseph's Tucson tailoring business was already well established. In 1881 he formed a partnership with Theresa's brother as Ferrin & Marx, Merchant Tailor and Clothing, and ran advertisements proclaiming, "You need not go outside of Tucson for your clothes when you can get a stylish fit here at San Francisco prices." The Ferrin family lived behind the shop in a modest adobe home at the corner of Meyer and Cushing Streets. Over time, the couple added an additional storefront. Within the first five years of her marriage, Theresa gave birth to three children: Hattie, Clara, and Arthur.

She became known as the lady with the healing herbs who helped local physician, Dr. John C. Handy. When Dr. Handy became the first chancellor of the University of Arizona in 1886, prior to its opening in 1891, he needed someone like Theresa to look after his patients. According to her grandson, Theresa "had come from Germany with knowledge of herbal and natural remedies…and helped nurse many sick townspeople back to health."

Her knowledge of medicinal cures earned her the reputation as a community healer. Many called her the "Angel of Tucson" for her ability to pull a remedy out of her bag, or out of her garden, to soothe a fevered brow or ease the pain of a broken bone. She almost always had a preparation or treatment for the variety of sicknesses, infections, contagions, and injuries that were prevalent in the small desert town. Her daughter Clara dreaded the sound of the buggy that came to take her mother away in the middle of the night "to nurse some sick friends." Theresa "was always at the beck & call of the sick and needy… Dr. Handy called her his best friend."

Along with her nursing abilities, Clara remembered her mother as an excellent cook who was "especially noted for her twelve-egg lemon pies." She probably purchased many of her fresh fruits and vegetables from the Chinese farmers who brought their produce into town each day. The butcher also knocked on her door so that Theresa, and other housewives, could place their daily orders. A local rancher supplied butter and eggs. With no refrigeration or ice, very little was kept from one day to the next. Earthenware pots called *ollas* (pronounced OY-ahs), were used to keep water cool by wrapping wet gunnysacks around the containers.

Theresa's leadership in the local Pioneer Society helped keep the organization afloat. "The [Pioneer Society] banquet and ball held each year was the event even we children looked forward to attending," Clara wrote. "Roast turkeys, suckling pigs, ham, great mounds of potato salad, to say nothing of the dozens of homemade cakes weighed down the long tables. As the evening advanced we were put to sleep on the wooden benches around the hall. Tucson was like one big family."

At the time, however, the streets of Tucson were replete with saloons but offered few places to worship. The majestic Mission San Xavier del Bac rose against the desert sky a few miles south of town, but only a small number of other religious establishments existed within the community. The Jewish population had no temple in which to hold services.

Theresa held Friday night and holy days services in her home while also taking care of the Torah, a significant honor representative of her standing in the community.

In 1890 a group of women gathered to organize the Hebrew Ladies Benevolent Society. As president of the society, Theresa became the driving force behind fund-raising efforts to build a temple of worship for Tucson's Jewish population. Such an undertaking was enormous in a town where the mainstream population

THERESA MARX FERRIN

KATHERINE RUTH BEARD

[1908~1998]

In the early 1930s, Katherine Ruth Beard showed up on the Navajo reservation with one suitcase, very little money, and a driving ambition to bring the Word of God to the people of the desert. She ministered to the Hopi and Navajo, traipsing over unmarked trails from one hogan to another, tending to the sick and burying the dead, but always caring for the religious needs of those who would listen.

For more than sixteen years, she worked at the Navajo Gospel Mission just north of the Hopi community of Oraibi. When her health faltered, she moved to Flagstaff and ran a small storefront mission.

As Indians from all tribes flocked into Flagstaff during World War II, the city asked Katherine to run an Indian center. "Of course, I would have Gospel services and Bible studies in the center every day," she said, "and I could deal directly with the Navajos in their own tongue. I couldn't do that with the other tribes, but most of them could understand English pretty well."

Her labors bore fruit when she started the Little Indian Bible Church north of the Sixth Army Ammunition Depot just outside of Flagstaff. In 1948 Katherine and many benefactors established the Flagstaff Mission to the Navajos.

She acquired land north of Flagstaff and built chapels closer to the reservation. Well into her eighties, Katherine continued to ride across the desert, bringing her ministry to hundreds of isolated Navajo and Hopi families. "The people are there," she counseled, "but you have to go out and find them."

consisted of ranchers, cowboys, miners, and a handful of shopkeepers, a virtual melting pot of citizenry from all over the country.

With daughter Clara in tow, Theresa scoured the town seeking donations, speaking to civic groups, and writing letters encouraging donations for the first Jewish temple in the territory.

On March 10, 1910, she watched proudly as the cornerstone was laid for the Temple Emanu-El. The magnificent building was not quite complete that October to celebrate Rosh Hashanah, but services were conducted in the new facility anyway. The Stone Avenue Temple, as it was originally called, was the culmination of Theresa's philanthropic work in the rugged Tucson community. The rounded windows and twin towers of the old temple have weathered the ravages of time, although the original stained-glass windows are long gone. In 1949 the last service was held in the old edifice. Today it is home to the Jewish History Museum. The temple is listed on the National Register of Historic Places.

Shortly after Temple Emanu-El's dedication, Theresa took ill and never had the opportunity to worship in the structure she had worked so hard to establish. She died February 24, 1911. The family home is now one of Tucson's finest dining establishments, the Cushing Street Bar & Restaurant. Approaching the restaurant, a little imagination can envision Theresa standing at the corner entrance inviting the Jewish community into her home for services. As the "Angel of Tucson," she saw to the physical as well as spiritual needs of the small desert town.

GOD'S HEROINE

St. Katharine (Catherine Hookey Drexel)

[1858–1955]

When Catherine Hookey Drexel was born November 26, 1858, few would have predicted what an incredible future was in store for this privileged child. A family of affluence and status, the Drexels of Philadelphia were known for their business acumen as well as their philanthropic deeds. Kate, as she was called during her childhood, was the second of three girls born to her father. Her mother died five months after Kate's birth, and her father eventually remarried and had another daughter from that union. Young Kate enjoyed all the frills of the well-to-do. Yet as devout Catholics, the Drexels also knew it was their duty to support those less fortunate. Kate believed it was her destiny to provide education for the most downtrodden of the races—the Native Americans of the Southwest and the African Americans in the southland.

Her compassion for the indigent started early, when she helped her stepmother conduct Sunday school classes for African American children in their posh Philadelphia home. Her first excursion west in 1884 left her with a lifelong desire to establish missions and schools for struggling Native Americans.

Upon the death of their father in 1885, the daughters became three of the wealthiest women in the country, with combined assets around $14 million. Already making charitable donations to Indian missions, Katharine (as she became known in her adult life) and her sisters were delighted to accept the invitation of Bishop James O'Connor, Katharine's spiritual adviser, and Father Joseph Stephan, director of the Bureau of Catholic Indian Missions, to head west in the fall of 1887.

Traveling to Indian reservations required stamina and a strong constitution, as no railroads spanned the desolate regions occupied by most tribes. By buckboard the party made its way to the Rosebud School in South Dakota, a product of Katharine's generosity. In Pine Bluff, the sisters met Red Cloud, one of the most important chiefs among the Sioux. Katharine had contributed to the building of a mission in Stephan, South Dakota, and was treated to an Indian dance not usually witnessed by outsiders.

She headed west again the following year to visit the Chippewa in Red Lake, Minnesota, and an Indian boarding school run by Benedictine sisters in White Earth, Montana. She was already sponsoring twenty-two missions and subsidizing many others.

In 1889 Katharine left her worldly life behind to enter the Sisters of Mercy order as a novitiate. As she donned the plain dress and veil she would wear for the next six months, she could not help but reveal a little of the extravagant lifestyle she had known all her life. "You would be pleased with my veil," she wrote her sisters, "which is of lace quite as fine and pretty as my Paris lace dress..."

In February 1891 she left the Sisters of Mercy to start her own congregation, the Sisters of the Blessed Sacrament for Indians and Colored People, and began construction on a new convent in Cornwell Heights (now Bensalem), Pennsylvania. St. Elizabeth's was completed in 1892. Starting her own congregation allowed Katharine, now known as Reverend Mother Katharine, to maintain control over her personal finances instead of turning her capital over to the Church. Prejudice against Indians and blacks left her wary that her efforts to provide funds to those who truly needed her intervention would be ignored.

She continued to visit the western schools her vast fortune helped establish. In 1895 she purchased two hundred acres in an area known as La Cienega Amarilla, just west of the Arizona/New Mexico border, with the purpose of starting a school for Navajo children.

She made her first trip into Navajo country in 1900 to check on the planned school and returned the following year to meet with respected Navajo elders to assure them the school she called St. Michael would soon be open. Construction was well under way and Katharine was pleased with the progress, although the corn crop had failed. She had wanted to fill the children's mattresses with dried corn husks, but a dry season made the husks unfit for use. She and the other sisters tried stuffing the mattresses with wool but even after several washings, the wool still smelled like mutton and was discarded.

To ensure the school would become self-sufficient, she purchased additional land for farming next to St. Michael and hired Charley Zoo to plow the acreage. According to one report, a Mr. McJunken showed up claiming he owned the property and demanding to be compensated. When he provided no proof of ownership, Katharine refused to hand over any money. One day he confronted Katharine as Charley Zoo came into view. When McJunken saw the Navajo farmer, he hightailed to parts unknown. It turned out that Charley was known as much for his sharpshooting as for his farming abilities.

On October 15, 1902, Sister Mary Evangelist from the Sisters of the Blessed Sacrament boarded a train out of Philadelphia for Santa Fe. She would become the first Mother Superior of St. Michael School. Katharine, who was already in the West, met up with her along with sisters Mary Angela and Mary Agatha, and the assemblage headed for Gallup.

From Gallup, the five-hour buckboard ride to the reservation was as bone jolting as trying to stay on a bucking bronco, yet Sister Agatha found the rough trail exhilarating. "During the long ride we saw four crows, two wagons and a few Indians. I think we enjoyed it very much as there was a great deal of laughing done, making up prayers in between times. We were almost pure white with dust, at least our shawls and veils were, and the sun poured down on us, but we were not the least troubled, because we were on the way to the Navajo."

The sisters spent their first night at St. Michael on the floor of the unfinished, three-story schoolhouse. The next day they followed workmen from room to room, washing windows and hanging curtains in preparation for the school's opening. Six more sisters arrived from St. Elizabeth's. By mid-November, the sisters occupied six rooms on the lower floor until the second floor convent was completed. Almost every day freight wagons pulled into the remote district with an abundance of equipment and furnishings. According to Father Anselm

Weber, one of the Franciscan priests who had been sent to teach at the school, Katharine paid for everything, "even for horses and saddles and Mass wine."

"Home for us was this new unfinished school of St. Michael," wrote one of the sisters, "where we were to wait—wait for the children of the desert to come."

On December 3, 1902, Feast Day of St. Francis Xavier, High Mass at St. Michael was conducted by Father Bernard Haile. In attendance besides Katharine and the sisters were the first twenty-four students to enroll in the school. Just three months earlier, when the first postal service was inaugurated at La Cienega, the region officially became known as St. Michaels, Arizona Territory.

Even while in the East, Katharine kept a keen eye on the doings at the school. She asked copious questions and offered helpful suggestions. "Please estimate how many tons of coal you will need this year and how does the range burn? What do you think of a fence made of stumps set on end? Put zinc in the back of the pot closet and then you can move it out and examine it for roaches."

School enrollment increased steadily through the years as more students from neighboring tribes found their way to St. Michael. They were not without their share of troubles, such as the 1911 measles outbreak that left two students dead, and a flash flood a few years later that destroyed the school's gardens and storage buildings. All but two pigs were lost. In 1920 the influenza epidemic that spread around the world made its way to St. Michaels, infecting more than eighty children. All but one recovered.

Yet there were also times of great fun, such as a baseball game Katharine attended between the soldiers at Fort Defiance and St. Michael employees. "Can you imagine me taking an interest in baseball?" she wrote. As the score remained close, two of the sisters headed for the chapel with one of them remarking, "This is going to require some very serious praying." And sure enough, Katharine affirmed, "prayer won the game."

The gardens at the school produced bountiful repasts—string beans, cabbage, cucumbers, potatoes, watermelon; there was even fresh milk from the cow. "Best of all," according to Katharine, "is the crop of souls." She was overjoyed that forty-six Navajos had been baptized during the first three years of the mission.

Katharine expanded her educational territory by funding tuition for Tohono O'odham children to attend schools in Window Rock and on the Gila River Reservation. She also supported schools and churches at Anegam, Comobadi, and Pachemo on the Tohono O'odham Reservation; a Yaqui church south of Tucson; and the Yaquis' San Ignacio de Loyola at Chuama. She paid the salaries of teachers at San Xavier del Bac Mission School.

Her involvement with African American communities was just as intense as the work she performed with Native Americans. Along with millions of dollars

ST. KATHARINE (CATHERINE HOOKEY DREXEL)

in donations, she built St. Francis de Sales Girls School along the banks of the James River in Virginia; Immaculate Mother Academy for black girls in Nashville, Tennessee; St. Monica School in Chicago; and Xavier University in New Orleans, Louisiana, the first all-black Catholic college in the United States.

Even as her health failed, she refused to slow down, making her last trip west in 1935. She spent her remaining years as an invalid at St. Elizabeth's convent, the home she had built for the Sisters of the Blessed Sacrament for Indians and Colored People, in Bensalem, Pennsylvania.

On March 3, 1955, Reverend Mother Katharine Drexel died at the convent. At the time of her death, there were 502 professed Sisters of the Blessed Sacrament, thirty novices, and eight postulates serving at forty-eight convents and sixty institutions comprising forty-eight elementary schools, twelve high schools, and one university. Although she kept terrible financial records, it is estimated she spent more than $20 million during her lifetime to teach the indigent and downtrodden.

At her wake, one man held up his son and told the boy, "Take a look at the nun, son. Some day you can say that you looked upon a saint."

Katharine's cause for canonization was introduced in Rome in 1964. In January 1987, she was declared venerable by Pope John Paul II.

Reverend Mother Katharine Drexel was beatified by Pope John Paul II in November 1988. Native Americans appeared in Rome to pay homage to the woman who had given their children a chance to learn and thrive in the modern world. Eagle Dancers from the Laguna tribe performed at the altar, and Marie Tso Allen spoke the first Navajo ever used in a Vatican liturgy.

To achieve sainthood, two miracles have to be attributed to an individual. Young Amy Wall had been born deaf. After her family prayed to Katharine, the child could hear. Fourteen-year-old Robert Gutherman suffered a severe ear infection that could have cost him his life and most certainly his hearing. Again, the family prayed to Katharine and the infection subsided. Both of these phenomena could not be explained by physicians and were ruled miracles attributed to Katharine's intervention. She was formally canonized on October 1, 2000. Saint Katharine's feast day is March 3.

As one Philadelphia newspaper reported at the time of Katharine's death, "She belongs so truly to all America, but especially to the poor and forgotten people of the land—our Indians and Negroes. She was indeed a heroine of God."

A DAMN GOOD DOCTOR

Florence Brookhart Yount

[1909–1988]

Dr. Florence Brookhart Yount loved history as much as she loved medicine. She could tell you what was going on in Prescott in the 1800s just as easily as she could count how many babies she delivered in a year. She frequently delighted audiences with the history of territorial medicine, including when and where Prescott's first hospitals appeared and how the Methodist Church got its start in Prescott. Her own history in this central Arizona town touched many lives, and she is still remembered as the lady doctor who delivered and looked after "Grade A babies."

Born in Washington, Iowa, March 5, 1909, Florence and her family relocated to Washington D.C. in 1927, after her father Smith Brookhart had won a seat in the U.S. Senate five years prior.

A cosmopolitan young woman, Florence was often seen riding around the nation's capital in her sporty roadster. She had an avid curiosity for science, and by 1935, the striking twenty-three-year-old with soft brown hair, captivating dark eyes, and compelling smile had graduated from George Washington University and Medical School. She was one of five women in her class, all that were allowed by university rules. One of the other eighty-eight medical students was Clarence Edgar "Ned" Yount Jr. from Prescott, Arizona. Together, Florence and Ned interned at a Washington D.C. hospital where she remembered delivering seven babies in one night.

On June 22, 1936, the couple married at the Brookhart family home in Iowa, then headed to Prescott for their honeymoon.

Florence's new in-laws had been part of Prescott's medical community since 1902, when Dr. C. E. Yount Sr. came to town to recover from tuberculosis. Ned began practicing with his father while Florence headed to Children's Hospital in Chicago to complete a residency program in pediatrics. Her friends warned her about the dangers of Chicago "mobs," and Florence soon realized her home was right in the middle of gangster territory. "But it didn't matter," she said. "We were on duty twenty-four hours a day."

Returning to Prescott, she opened her practice in the offices of her father-in-law and husband. Prejudice against woman doctors was still quite prevalent, but she had no time to worry about those who would not accept her. "I always felt 'that's your problem—not mine,'" she said as she headed off to deliver another new Prescott citizen.

FLORENCE BROOKHART YOUNT

She was known as "Doctor Pat" when she visited the homes of her maternity patients. Emergencies involving children at the county hospital always sent her flying out the door. Pay was not important. Local quarrymen sometimes brought her flagstones as compensation for delivering their newborn son or daughter.

During the Great Depression, Florence instituted a well-baby clinic. She had learned at Chicago's Children's Hospital that a well-balanced, nourishing meal often meant drugs would not be necessary. "We gave out enormous amounts of canned milk. Every week, we'd weigh babies, check them, give them shots and vitamins. This was Depression times. One day we had as many as thirty babies."

She followed the children she brought into the world throughout their young lives, even attending football games at the local high school if one of her kids was playing. "I did have lots of Grade A babies," she once remarked.

The hospital situation in Prescott was not in good shape when Florence arrived. The Sisters of St. Joseph ran the first hospital in town, but it only lasted ten years. In 1893 the Sisters of Mercy founded a small hospital in a vacant house. The modern facility they built in 1903 burned to the ground in 1940.

Many women opened their homes to patients, particularly to expectant mothers from rural communities who came into town near their delivery dates. Registered nurse Catherine Lennox took in pregnant women as well as accident patients. Florence gave birth to her own son John Edward Yount at Catherine's home on September 6, 1940. New father Ned, who was in the National Guard and on his way to the South Pacific, "brought me home…and left an hour later."

Having two physicians in the family, John remembered as a child he "didn't dare get sick," and he never missed a day of school.

During World War II, most of the doctors left to serve in the military. Florence, her father-in-law, and a few older physicians took care of Prescott's growing population during their absence, and her obstetrics practice flourished. "I delivered seven hundred or more babies before the men doctors got back, and by then it was a habit," she said.

She took particular pride in her work with premature infants. Her son John remembered seeing her take off her wedding rings and putting them on an extremely tiny baby's wrists like bracelets.

During the War, the need for a modern hospital became even more imperative. An old vacant elementary school attracted Florence and others who thought it would suffice as a health care center, if they could raise the $10,000 necessary to convert it into a workable facility. "We had to work hard to generate the spirit for a community hospital," she said. These were difficult times, "[b]ut everybody did rally."

Medical equipment was hard to find, as most of it went to the war effort. Florence heard of an old stove gathering dust at the abandoned Golden Turkey Mine near what is now the ghost town of Cleator. Jumping into her car, she used her own rationed gasoline to haul it back to Prescott, where it was installed in the new hospital.

On March 1, 1943, Prescott Community Hospital opened its doors. That evening, Florence delivered the first baby at the new facility.

Catherine Lennox took over as the first superintendent of nursing and, along with Florence, convinced older nurses to come out of retirement, ensuring the hospital would have a superior nursing staff.

When the polio epidemic swept across the country in the mid-1940s, Florence helped institute a campaign to inoculate everyone in Yavapai County. "Doctors all worked on that so we could say every person in the county could have that protection."

In 1949 she joined the Arizona State Board of Public Welfare to help manage the distribution of grants to programs that assisted crippled children, Indian children, the aged, and the blind. It was a stormy time for Florence. She resigned in 1951 after accusing the board of ignoring the needs of those they served. "Tossing around programs involving crippled children, blind people, and the aged needy on a political bargain counter is utterly repulsive to me," she stormed.

In 1973 at age sixty-four, she retired from practicing medicine and devoted her time to studying the history of Prescott, one of Arizona's oldest towns, and the history of medicine. She particularly enjoyed discovering some of the medical remedies that were prevalent in the 1800s.

"We have in our home the medicine chest that served the Younts a hundred years ago," she reminisced. "It is full of stationery at the moment, but if you bring your nose close enough you can still smell the quinine."

More than sixty years of experience in the Yount family, including her own thirty years, gave Florence wisdom and insight into the medical field. Mothers, she said, were often the only doctors around. They collected and dried particular leaves for teas that eased many pains, and grew herbs for specific illnesses.

In her own fields of obstetrics and pediatrics, she discovered that at one time it was considered beneficial to boil one's wedding rings and drink the tea to alleviate a difficult labor. And someone once professed that if a person would "hold the sharp edge of an axe against the abdomen of a woman in labor, [i]t will take her mind off her troubles." Babies stood a better chance of growing straight and tall if they were dressed from the feet up, while earaches could be cured by dipping black sheep's wool in rum and putting it in the little tyke's ear.

Florence was part of the effort to establish the Territorial Women's Memorial Rose Garden at Prescott's Sharlot Hall Museum that "is dedicated to those women of Arizona who prepared the way for others." She also participated in acquiring Governor John C. Fremont's old house and restoring it on the museum grounds.

Florence died November 25, 1988. Her son once remarked that when she first began practicing with her husband and father-in-law, many assumed she was the nurse in the office. "She wasn't a nurse, she was a doctor," he said, "and a damn good one."

WOMEN ENTREPRENEURS

Women have always been in business of one type or another, and their enterprises have had a remarkable impact on the nation. From small cottage industries to giant conglomerates, they have competed in American industry by developing a variety of successful and sometimes unique ventures. This was particularly true during the early westward movement, as women often had to devise means to retain their homes and feed their children after a spouse died or abandoned the family.

After divorcing her husband, African American Elizabeth Smith successfully ran the Vernetta Hotel in Wickenburg until the national spread of racial prejudice turned the community against her. With only the help of her three strapping sons, Angela Hammer owned and ran newspapers from Wickenburg to Casa Grande, becoming the first female newspaperwoman in Arizona Territory.

Many women opened their homes to lodgers, while others successfully ran boardinghouses and restaurants, as did Nellie Cashman, who fed and sheltered miners in Tucson and Tombstone, as well as the far reaches of Alaska, earning a reputation as the "Miner's Angel."

Sarah Bowman, a shrewd businesswoman with a tarnished reputation, traveled with the military as cook and laundress in the 1850s, when Arizona was still part of New Mexico Territory. When she stayed put long enough, she opened and managed hotels and restaurants and never turned a sorry soul from her doorstep.

Married women often joined their husbands in enterprises beyond the home front. Louisa Wetherill and her husband ran the Kayenta Trading Post in northern Arizona for more than thirty years, developing a strong, lasting relationship with the native people as they fostered understanding of customs and practices unfamiliar to the Anglo way of life.

Today, women are an integral part of the business world in a myriad of professions. Their futures know no bounds.

POTS, PANS, AND PROSTITUTES

Sarah Bowman

[CIRCA 1813–1866]

Just one thin sheet of sandpaper separated Yuma from Hell, according to Sarah Bowman, a giant of a woman who followed the U.S. Army across Texas and Mexico before settling in this isolated desert spot along the Colorado River. Over six feet tall and weighing close to two hundred pounds, the buxom red-haired beauty earned the reputation as a hard-working astute businesswoman, even though she could neither read nor write. She did learn to speak fluent Spanish, however. Toiling as a laundress and cook for the military, her status among the soldiers was one of awe and fear. One of them reported her as a "[r]emarkably large, well proportioned, strong woman of strong nerves and great physical power, capable of enduring great fatigue." Another christened her the "Great Western" after one of the largest steam-powered ships to cross the Atlantic Ocean.

Sarah Bowman first appeared traveling with General Zachary Taylor's army as they made their way into disputed territory along the banks of the Rio Grande in 1846. Supposedly married to one of the soldiers, she was listed as a laundress for the military. Where she came from remains a mystery. Reports list her birth sometime between 1812 and 1817 in either Tennessee or Missouri.

As battle raged around Fort Texas (later Fort Brown) that April, Sarah took her pots and pans, headed to the center of the fort, and set up her kitchen. These boys would not be without strong hot coffee and a nourishing meal if she had anything to say about it. Allowed to charge for her services, she asked nothing for her meals while the fort was under siege.

For seven days and nights the conflict continued. Sarah requested a musket so she could replace those who had fallen. "[T]he cannonballs, bullets and shot... were falling thick and fast around her," read one military report. "She continued to administer to the wants of the wounded and dying; at last the siege became so hot that a bullet passed through her bonnet and another through her bread tray."

When the smoke cleared, Taylor moved his troops across the river to Matamoros, Mexico, where Sarah set up what became the first of her many boardinghouses along the military road.

By September both Taylor and Sarah were in Monterrey, after surviving a bloody four-day battle to take the town. She worked in the field with one of the doctors, carrying away the wounded and serving coffee to the troops.

To supplement her laundress wages, she opened the American House hotel in Monterrey, providing all the necessities a battle-scarred soldier could desire—food, liquor, and the company of obliging women. Yet when Taylor headed toward the town of Saltillo that November, she packed up and moved with him, establishing another American House. One soldier said he "paid $2.50 for my entertainment at the boarding house of the Great Western."

Some of Taylor's troops deserted during a particularly bloody battle, and one of the fugitives made his way back to the American Hotel, proclaiming Taylor was going down in defeat. Sarah, who absolutely adored Zachary Taylor, soundly punched the man in the face. "You damned son of a bitch," she shouted, "there ain't Mexicans enough in Mexico to whip old Taylor. You just spread that report and I'll beat you to death." Those who witnessed the confrontation quickly returned to the battlefield.

The U.S.–Mexican War lasted two years, ending when U.S. troops withdrew in the summer of 1848. As the forces headed for California, Sarah asked to go along, but was refused since she was no longer married to a military man.

Sarah went by several last names during her lifetime, as husbands, or the appearance of a husband, were a necessary encumbrance if she wanted to remain with the army. She immediately set out to find her next spouse. Riding down a line of soldiers, she announced, "Who wants a wife with fifteen thousand dollars, and the biggest leg in Mexico! Come my beauties, don't all speak at once—who is the lucky man?" A soldier named Davis accepted the offer if a clergyman could be found to make the union official. "Bring your blanket to my tent tonight," Sarah laughed, "and I will learn you to tie a knot that will satisfy you I reckon!"

In the spring of 1849 she was running a hotel on the north side of the Rio Grande in a small community called Ponce's Ranch that would later become the town of El Paso.

According to one biography of her life, she showed up next in 1850 in Socorro, New Mexico, with five orphaned children. Whether the Skinner youngsters lost their parents on the way west is unknown, but Sarah took them under her wing. Nancy Skinner remained with Sarah for many years and was heard to call her "Mother."

By this time, she had also acquired another husband, having left the newlywed Davis along the road somewhere. German-born Albert Bowman was a military man and remained with Sarah longer than her other conquests, although there is no record they ever married. When he was discharged from the army in late 1852, the couple headed for the gold fields of California. They made it as far as Fort Yuma.

Having relocated to its present site in early 1852 under the leadership of Major Samuel Peter Heintzelman, Fort Yuma sat atop a hill on the California side of the Colorado River. Sarah signed on to cook for the officers. Although Heintzelman found the big woman objectionable, his men swarmed around her and offered her good pay to clean and cook for them. The major kept his distance but jealously noted in his journal, "The Western, as she calls herself, had a dinner yesterday and everybody in camp but me was invited. She sent to me for butter."

Eventually, Heintzelman succumbed to Sarah's charms and soon became one of her staunchest supporters, dining with her regularly. "I sent the Western a couple of nice watermelons for our dinner," he noted in his journal.

That March, Heintzelman reported that Sarah came to him claiming someone was trying to take two orphan girls from her. One of these girls was Nancy Skinner from New Mexico. To protect the children, Sarah moved across the river into Sonora with Heintzelman's help, although he wrote in his journal, "I can't see what she expects to do for a living when she moves over there."

Always the entrepreneur, Sarah knew exactly what she was doing. If she stayed at the fort, she had to abide by army rules and that hurt her business, so she may have come up with this ruse about the children in order to ply her trade as she wished. Still close enough to the fort for the soldiers to enjoy their free time at Sarah's place, she offered, as usual, good food, strong whiskey, and willing women.

Heintzelman soon realized Sarah had made him her fool. "The Western is making a convenience of us…" he wrote. "She gives us what she pleases to eat and spends the whole day across the river." No one seemed to mind but the Major.

In December 1853 the United States bought 45,000 square miles of land from Mexico. Congress ratified the Gadsden Treaty on June 30, 1854. This purchase put Sarah's house in the U.S., in New Mexico Territory. In 1863, when the western half of New Mexico Territory became Arizona Territory, Sarah became the first Anglo woman to live in and run a business in the town of Yuma, AT (Arizona Territory).

As Fort Yuma grew, Sarah and Albert Bowman agreed to supply adobe bricks for the construction of public buildings. Signing a contract to make 700,000 adobe bricks, Sarah marked the agreement with her "X." Throughout all her dealings with the army, she never learned to write.

On February 22, 1856, eighteen-year-old Olive Ann Oatman walked into Fort Yuma after surviving five years in Indian captivity. Most of the Oatman family had been massacred along the Gila River in 1851 by an unidentified Indian tribe. Olive and her younger sister Mary Ann were taken captive. Mary Ann died of starvation, but Olive survived and was finally sold back to her people for the price of one horse. When she was returned to the fort, it was Sarah who took

SARAH BOWMAN

her in and cared for the young woman until her brother Lorenzo, who had miraculously survived the massacre, came for her.

Seeing a future in the bustling town of Tucson, Sarah and Albert left Yuma in the fall of 1856 to open a boardinghouse in the Old Pueblo. By the following spring, however, Sarah, whose trade depended on the military, moved her business to the newly established Fort Buchanan, forty miles south of Tucson near the Sonoita River.

Ten-year-old Jeff Ake lived near Fort Buchanan and remembered Sarah's place of business in Patagonia. "She packed two six-shooters, and they all said she shore could use 'em. That she had killed a couple of men in her time." His father Felix once called Sarah "the greatest whore in the West."

By 1860, she was back in Yuma. The census that year listed three children living with her.

At the onset of the Civil War, troops were pulled out of western outposts and sent to the East. Sarah moved back into Fort Yuma, which had little to do with the fighting except to house troops passing through. One young recruit noted his first visit from Sarah.

At the time of arrival at the Fort, Feb, 1863, as I was sitting in front of my room trying to eliminate some of the dust acquired during my 300 miles tramp; I was accosted by a large American woman, a six footer, and proportionately broad with: "Lieutenant have you any washing you want done?" I hastened to hand her the only change of shirts I had. I enquired who she was and was informed she was the best known woman in the American Army… "The Great Western." … She was a splendid example of the American frontier woman.

Although most soldiers and prospectors were upstanding citizens, Fort Yuma had its share of deserters and ne'er-do-wells. Thievery became so rampant in 1864 that everyone was under scrutiny. Although Sarah was not suspected of stealing from the army, she gave a deposition that proved damning for several officers. She testified officials told her to supply miners with military goods whenever they asked, adding, "It was almost an every day thing to see Mules, and 'burrows' packing Flour away from the Post…"

In her deposition, she also stated she had served as hospital matron at the fort for more than ten years, adding to her list of occupations as cook, laundress, hotel and restaurant owner, madam, and heroine.

Sarah, no longer living with Albert Bowman, was probably in her early fifties when she died on December 23, 1866. No record of how she died exists, but one officer claimed she succumbed to a tarantula or spider bite. She was the only woman ever buried in the Fort Yuma Cemetery.

"Blunt and unguarded in speech," reported the *Arizona Gazette*, "she was yet the possessor of a kind heart, and whatever her failings, engendered by wild associations, very many will remember with grateful feeling the acts of tenderness bestowed by her on themselves and associated in that inhospitable section. Always at the bedside of the sick, she cared for them as none but a woman can and nothing that money or care could furnish was neglected by her."

In 1890 the old Yuma cemetery was in great disrepair. The 159 bodies buried there were re-interred at the San Francisco National Cemetery, Presidio. Sarah went with the troops, as she had throughout her life.

BOARDINGHOUSES AND BOOMTOWNS

Nellie Cashman

[CIRCA 1845–1925]

ngel of Tombstone," "Frontier Angel," the "Miner's Angel," "Savior in the Wilderness," and "Saint of Sourdoughs"—the latter a term related to early settlers and prospectors in Alaska. All of these names have been bestowed upon a little Irish lass with a resonant brogue who set up boardinghouses, staked mining claims from Mexico to Alaska, fed ravished miners, helped the downtrodden, and raised thousands of dollars for charitable causes.

There had never been anyone like Nellie Cashman on the western frontier when she showed up in the late 1800s. No one ever questioned her respectability as she mingled with miners, catered to gamblers, and aided convicts. She could get a boardinghouse open and running within a matter of days, and her ability to prepare and serve appetizing and affordable meals lasted over fifty years.

Nellie was born in Midleton, County Cork, Ireland, probably in 1845. The only evidence of her birth is a baptismal record dated October 15 of that year. At the age of five, she immigrated with her widowed mother and younger sister Fanny to Boston. When she was about twenty years old, the threesome headed for San Francisco.

After her sister Fanny married Tom Cunningham, Nellie and her mother left San Francisco to run the Miner's Boarding House in the brawling mining district of Pioche, Nevada, advertising the hotel and restaurant as having a "table… supplied with the best to be had in the Market."

Prospecting became a passion for Nellie; she would go wherever a strike looked promising. Most mining communities had no decent place to eat or sleep. Nellie provided food and lodging in many of these rowdy camps. She prospected in the lucrative gold fields of Cassiar in the northwestern section of British Columbia in 1874 after setting up a boardinghouse and saloon and grubstaking a few prospectors down on their luck.

That November, just after she left Cassiar, an early winter storm stranded the remaining miners, cutting off their supply route. Scurvy soon ran rampant through the camp. Hiring a handful of men, Nellie purchased over fifteen hundred pounds of supplies and headed back into the winter storm to rescue the miners, who had become her friends. Her heroics made front-page headlines from St. Louis to San Francisco, and Nellie's reputation as the miner's angel was born.

When the Sisters of St. Ann in Victoria decided to build a hospital to care for ailing and injured miners, Nellie persuaded her fellow prospectors to open their bags of gold dust and donate to the cause. St. Joseph's Hospital became her haven through the years. She often visited the sisters when she needed a respite from the brutality and wickedness that pervaded some of the stark mining camps.

By June 1879, she had left the frozen frontier for the bawdy town of Tucson, advertising her Delmonico Restaurant as having "The Best Meals in the City." Yet by the following April, the lure of silver in Tombstone sent her down the road to try her luck searching for lucrative silvery veins. She operated the Nevada Boot & Shoe Store in Tombstone as well as the Tombstone Cash Store, which provided fresh fruits and vegetables to hungry mobs that descended on the town looking for productive strikes. That October she opened the Arcade Restaurant & Chop House.

Nellie was an integral part of the Tombstone community. Shortly after setting up her businesses, she began soliciting donations to build a Catholic church and county hospital to save the souls and bodies of desperate miners who rode into town seeking their fortunes.

"Nellie Cashman, the irrepressible, started out yesterday to raise funds for the building of a Catholic church," the *Tombstone Epitaph* announced in September 1880. "We…will bet that there is a Catholic church in Tombstone before many days if Nellie has to build it herself."

She begged, borrowed, and some say even stole from gamblers to acquire enough money for the church and hospital, shaming them into turning over lucrative gaming profits.

On November 28, 1880, Sacred Heart Church of Tombstone held its first services. The county hospital saw its first patients the following year.

Selling the Nevada Boot & Shoe Store along with the Arcade Restaurant, she next headed to the copper mines of Bisbee. Just three weeks after she left Tombstone, the town was in flames from an explosion at the Oriental Saloon, right next door to the Arcade Restaurant. She had sold out just in time.

She opened the Bisbee Hotel in July 1881, but the town did not flourish as anticipated and she was back in Tombstone by September, running the Russ House Hotel and Restaurant.

Fanny's husband died in February 1881. Nellie brought her sister and five small children to live with her in Tombstone, and by fall, she and Fanny were operating the Delmonico Lodging House.

But Fanny was not well, and Nellie had her hands full taking care of her sister and tending to five boisterous youngsters. She sold her businesses to concentrate on her sister's welfare. Once Fanny recovered, the sisters opened the American Hotel and Restaurant, where "elegant meals can be had at all hours."

In the spring of 1882 fire once again spread across Tombstone. The *Epitaph* reported, "the American Hotel, kept by Miss Cashman and Mrs. Cunningham, was in imminent danger. But the plucky ladies stationed several of their friends with buckets and kept the building thoroughly saturated with water, thereby preventing the flames from communicating."

Nellie acquired either ownership or a partnership in several mines around Tombstone, including the Big Blue claim in the Huachucha Mountains, the Last Chance claim in the Turquoise Mining District, the Littlefield and New Year claims in the Cochise area, and the Nellie mine plus a portion of the Big Comet mine near Tombstone. Her mining investments kept her solvent while her hotel and restaurant businesses waxed and waned. Regardless of her own financial situation, however, she could always be counted on to assist a down-and-out prospector.

The 1883 gold strike in Baja California prompted Nellie to lead a team of twenty-one Tombstone men 450 miles south of San Diego with the prospect of digging up a payload of bullion. The road was long, the desert merciless, and the discouraged miners returned to Tombstone empty-handed. Nellie reported she found no signs of gold, only cactus, rocks, and Spanish bayonet (yucca).

Newspapers reported that Nellie saved the lives of those who followed her into the Mexican desert by finding water before they perished. The *Weekly Arizona Citizen* praised her abilities in the face of danger, proclaiming this was "what an energetic and plucky woman can do."

NELLIE CASHMAN

Through the years, tales about the daring Nellie Cashman grew and became truths without proof. In all the interviews she gave after both of the following incidents, she never mentioned a word about either episode.

In December 1883 five men robbed a Bisbee store. In the ensuing melee, two bystanders were killed. The law quickly rounded up the outlaws, and tried and convicted them of the murders. As they lingered in the Tombstone jail, a circus-like atmosphere pervaded the town. Bleachers were built and tickets sold for the upcoming hangings.

Nellie, who felt the desperados deserved at least a dignified hanging, supposedly let her outrage be known by recruiting a handful of trusted cronies and arranging for the bleachers to suspiciously collapse the night before the hangings. The five men went to their deaths sans a bawdy spectacle.

The Frontier Angel is also credited with rescuing mining superintendent E. B. Gage during a labor dispute, by whisking him out of town before he could be lynched.

Fanny died of tuberculosis on July 3, 1884, leaving Nellie to rear the five Cunningham children. Michael Cunningham, the second-oldest of Fanny's children, who became a prominent citizen of Bisbee, recalled how Nellie handled this rough-and-tumble group, particularly the time he and another boy rode out of town just before dark. As blackness fell across the desert, nearby Indian fires blazed along the mountain ridges. The two boys hunkered down, fearing for their lives. When they heard a wagon rumbling toward them, they knew they were doomed. But there sat Aunt Nellie, unafraid of the pending peril. She had come to fetch her boy.

Childhood fistfights in front of her house sometimes resulted in mediation by Nellie and a slice of pie for the offenders. After a while, the fights were staged just to get some of that delicious pie.

She sometimes took the children with her as she made her way from one mining camp to another. She "worked like a Trojan in her search for riches," Michael recalled, "but she was constantly giving it away to the poor and needy and to various projects of her church." When he was old enough, Michael left his nomadic aunt "because I just couldn't keep up with her."

Back in Tombstone, Nellie was once again running the Russ House until January 1886, when she and a Mrs. Pauline Jones took up residence in Nogales, announcing they were opening the Delmonico Hotel and Restaurant with "the best table in the territory" including "the finest Liquors and Cigars." Gold and silver had been found in the area, but not enough to warrant a steady stream of customers. The April 17, 1886, *Epitaph* reported, "Nellie Cashman has sold her hotel at Nogales."

By summer she was in Tucson running the dining room of the Palace Hotel. Tucson, however, had become too cosmopolitan for Nellie, and she headed back to Tombstone, partnering with a couple of prospectors to locate the Miners Dream claim. Within a short time, she was off to the silver mines in Kingston, New Mexico. Opening the Cashman House, Nellie stayed through most of 1888 before closing up shop and heading back to Tucson and Tombstone.

When gold was discovered west of Phoenix in the Harqua Hala District, she showed up with groceries to sell while she worked on her own mining claims. By her own description, she considered these mines some of the most lucrative, "for this is the finest and largest ledge of exceedingly rich gold ore I have ever seen and if it should hold out to proposed depth this mine alone will make as good a mining town as Tombstone or Bodie [California] ever were."

She may have had her only romantic fling in Harqua Hala. The Phoenix *Daily Herald* reported on February 23, 1889, "Mike Sullivan, of the owners of the Bonanza mine at the Harqua Hala camp, left there yesterday in company with Miss Nellie Cashman, on their way to the nearest station where a minister could be obtained, in order to be made man and wife."

Whatever happened between the two lovers was not reported, and Nellie never mentioned her romantic interlude.

After leaving Harqua Hala, she later reportedly spent some time prospecting in the African diamond district. By January 1890, she was in Prescott, and over the next few years, she may have traveled to California, Idaho, Wyoming, and Montana, prospecting wherever she thought she could dig up a profitable sum.

In the summer of 1894, she was running a hotel and restaurant for the copper miners in Jerome, but was gone by December.

Back in Prescott, she started the Elite Restaurant, but closed it within two months.

She trekked from Juneau, Alaska, to Sonora, Mexico, until February 1896, when she was back in Arizona running the Buffalo Hotel and Restaurant in Globe, advertising a "table of excellent quality." When one of the more profitable smelters closed down, however, she was off to Yuma, opening the Hotel Cashman in July 1897, with "meals on the European and American plan, table unsurpassed." This was Nellie's last venture in Arizona.

"Going to Alaska! I should say I am," she announced in an 1897 interview. Her years in the frozen tundra continued as they had in Arizona—prospecting, running hotels and restaurants while soliciting funds to build hospitals and churches, and saving a few miners' lives along the way.

She visited Arizona occasionally, but never again set up shop in the territory that had claimed her for almost twenty years. In a 1924 interview, she said she left Arizona "when things began to be civilized..."

Nellie Cashman died at age 80 on January 4, 1925, at St. Joseph's Hospital in Victoria, British Columbia, the same institution for which she had solicited funds from prospectors to build almost fifty years earlier.

"The 'old sourdough' has passed on," reported the *Arizona Daily Star*, "leaving many records behind—pioneer of Arizona, the first woman prospector in Alaska, the world's champion musher—but better by far than all of these is the fact that she lived—lived and enjoyed adventures that is not given most the courage to taste."

FRIEND OF THE NAVAJO

Louisa Wade Wetherill

[1878–1945]

Navajo Chief Hoskinini trusted Louisa Wetherill as he did no other Anglo. She knew his language, customs, and beliefs and did not disparage his people. She traded fairly and helped heal them if their own medicine did not work. He considered her his granddaughter.

Louisa knew the Navajos intimately—lived among them, respected them, laughed and cried with them. They called her *Asthon Sosi*, "the Slim Woman."

As a child growing up in Mancos Valley, Colorado, Louisa Wade never dreamed she would one day call Indians her friends. She fervently feared warring Utes and Paiutes who frequently raided her Colorado community.

Among her neighbors was the Wetherill family, who arrived in Mancos Valley about the same time as the Wades. On March 17, 1896, eighteen-year-old Louisa Wade married thirty-year-old John Wetherill. Their first child, Benjamin Wade Wetherill, was born December 26, 1896, followed by Georgia Ida on January 17, 1898.

Louisa and John ventured from one trading post to another, eking out a living in the deserts of New Mexico, Utah, and Arizona, trading with the Paiute, Ute, and Navajo. Their first trading post was in Ojo Alamo, New Mexico Territory. From there they went to Chavis (also called Chavez) near Thoreau, New Mexico. In 1904, combining inventory from Ojo Alamo and Chavis, they took over the trading post at Pueblo Bonito, about halfway between Thoreau and Farmington, New Mexico.

During this time, they met Clyde Coville, a bookkeeper with a knack for trading. Clyde became an integral part of the Wetherills' lives, working and living with them until his death in 1945.

With John often absent running freight wagons and working at excavations, Louisa was responsible for trading with the Indians and soon learned to speak "trade Navajo," words used when bartering. She discovered the kind, gentle nature of these people, and her fear of Indians quickly dissipated as she became familiar with their language and traditions.

In February 1906 John ventured into Oljato, just north of the Utah-Arizona border in the northwest part of the Navajo Nation now known as the Four Corners area. He was met by the son of Hoskinini, Hoskinini Begay, who ordered John and his party to leave immediately. Winning over the Navajos with a big feast, John convinced Hoskinini and his son that a trading post in the area would provide much-needed staples for their people, as well as a place to trade their livestock and wares. Oljato was the first station the Wetherills owned outright.

As Louisa prepared for the 250-mile trip from Pueblo Bonito to Oljato, she knew they would be encountering some of the roughest terrain in the Southwest. It took three days to get to Gallup, New Mexico, where they loaded up supplies. From there, slogging through heavy mud from torrential March rains, Louisa detailed the trip in one of her notebooks:

> The mud got so bad we could only go two or three miles a day. The wagons would go down and had to be unloaded and pulled out by hitching all of the teams onto them. We could look back at night and see the smoke from the campfire we had made the night before but we did not worry, we just kept fighting. It took us eight days to cross the mountain. When we reached Chinlee we had smooth sailing as far as the mud was concerned but there was no road from there to Oljato the place for which we were headed. It was ninety miles away and we had to build the road across washes as we went.

Twenty days after they left Pueblo Bonito, the Wetherills arrived in Oljato.

John and Louisa worked on building their home throughout that first summer. The adobe and stone foundation held up walls made of juniper logs and a dirt roof.

Paiutes, Utes, and Navajos all traded at Oljato. Louisa's kindness permeated into the hogans as she greeted each Indian as a friend, listened to their stories, sympathized with their grievances, and respected their traditions.

Hoskinini became her best friend. He confided in Louisa and she honored his trust. When he died in 1909, he bequeathed all his possessions to her, but

LOUISA WADE WETHERILL

she did not feel worthy of keeping these treasures and distributed them among his family.

When Navajo medicine man Wolfkiller came to work for the Wetherills, he introduced Louisa to plants and herbs the Navajos reserved for medicinal purposes, along with those used for food. Her medicine chest eventually totaled more than three hundred specimens.

The Navajos collected vegetation for a variety of ailments, as well as plants used in ceremonies. Bee stings, backaches, stomachaches, and headaches might be cured if one used the right ingredient. One plant was smoked to relieve a snakebite, the flower of another used to ensure a healthy pregnancy and easy labor. Placing a particular root around a sheep's neck kept coyotes at bay, while another plant could charm a horse into running faster.

Wolfkiller also taught Louisa many of the old Navajo myths, legends, and songs that his grandfather had once told him. She translated some of these into English, and later, her grandchildren preferred to hear such tales as "The Woman Whose Nose Was Cut Off Twelve Times," "How the Raven Got His Coat," "Story of the First Lie," and "Creation of the Burro" rather than typical bedtime stories.

The designs and details of Navajo sandpaintings also fascinated Louisa. Drawn into the sand to ward off illness, these intricate paintings made from ground charcoal and pulverized sandstone in colors of red, yellow, and white, were destroyed soon after they had served their purpose. She developed a friendship with Yellow Singer (Sam Chief) and convinced the Navajo man to copy some of these paintings in crayon. The paintings were later reproduced in watercolor by Clyde Coville to preserve their integrity.

On August 14, 1909, Navajo and Paiute guides led John Wetherill and a crew of surveyors, archaeologists, and students to the natural rock span of Rainbow Bridge, the largest natural bridge in the world. Indians knew of the 278-foot span, formed by sandstone erosion from waters flowing from Navajo Mountain to the Colorado River, long before Wetherill's group came upon the natural wonder, but John and his party were credited with its discovery. Even John dismissed the idea he was the first to know of the bridge, admitting Louisa's Indian friends had told her about the giant arch at least a year prior.

In the fall of 1910, the Wetherills opened another trading post in Kayenta, a remote area of northern Arizona in the heart of Monument Valley. They lived out of tents and wagons until their rock house was completed. The couple entertained visiting notables such as western writer Zane Gray, who patterned some of the characters in his books after John and Louisa. Theodore Roosevelt also stopped by in 1913 after a mountain lion hunting excursion at the Grand Canyon.

Around this time, many tribal families were forced to send at least one of their children to the Tuba City Boarding School, where students were forbidden to speak their native tongue, given strange food to eat, and severely punished if they did not follow rules they barely understood. Shortly after Louisa witnessed conditions at the school and mistreatment of the children, she took a little Ute girl named Esther home with her, but she suffered from tuberculosis and soon died. Next, she brought home Betty, a frightened, malnourished Navajo youngster. Years later, Betty recalled the beatings the children endured at the school and the rotten food they were forced to eat. "They were very mean to us," she remembered. "When we'd run away, or even speak a word of Navajo, they'd just more or less beat us." A young Navajo girl named Fanny soon joined Betty at the trading post. Both girls took the last name Wetherill and called Louisa "Mother."

The Navajos asked Louisa to intervene with the government in an attempt to alleviate the horrible conditions at the school. She met with Department of Interior officials in Washington D.C., arguing for a more understanding administrative staff. Within a short time, the school superintendent was transferred and conditions at the facility greatly improved.

At the beginning of World War I, Louisa and Hoskinini Begay went from hogan to hogan asking the Navajos to contribute to the Red Cross. Families donated valuable sheep and goats. The sale of the livestock providing much-needed medicine and bandages for war casualties. Louisa received national recognition for her work during the Red Cross drive.

The influenza epidemic of 1918–1919 hit the Navajo Nation hard, afflicting both John and Louisa, along with hundreds of Indians. As soon as she was back on her feet, Louisa and her daughter tended to the Indians who came looking for aid against a disease their own medicine could not cure. Clyde Coville and John buried the dead.

Scientific excursions based out of the Kayenta Trading Post abounded during the 1920s, along with movie moguls who recognized that the magnificent giant sandstone mountains and the vastness of the desert provided perfect backgrounds for episodic adventures. Director John Huston and actor Andy Devine stayed at the Wetherill lodge while filming *Out West with Andy Hardy*. When Zane Gray's *The Vanishing American* was filmed around Monument Valley and Rainbow Bridge, Louisa served as technical advisor and designer of native costumes for the film.

As many as fifty people might sit down for dinner at Kayenta. Louisa entertained them all—visiting dignitaries, movie stars, tourists, and neighboring Indians who brought their pelts, blankets, silver, and turquoise to barter.

In 1924, while continuing to run the post at Kayenta during the summer months, John and Louise took over management of La Osa Ranch during the winter. About seventy miles south of Tucson, the old adobe building, built around 1881, had thirty-two rooms to accommodate Arizona visitors. While John escorted archaeologists and tourists around the state, Louisa catered to the needs of the cast and crew making a film version of Harold Bell Wright's novel, *The Son of His Father.*

La Osa was sold in 1928 and the Wetherills returned to Kayenta, continuing to welcome personalities such as Ansel Adams, whose celebrated photographs captured the beauty of the sand dunes and magnificent sunsets.

In 1943 a huge cloudburst turned nearby waters into a sea of mud that tore through the Kayenta lodge and trading post. Many of Louisa's papers, particularly the stories she had heard from Wolfkiller and translated into English, were destroyed. Never one to be distressed over what she considered a minor interruption, Louisa made her way through the mud and muck that oozed into her kitchen and rescued a roast she had put in the oven for dinner.

For over thirty years, John and Louisa ran the Kayenta Trading Post, living and working with the Navajo people. In 1944 seventy-eight-year-old John Wetherill died after trekking many a mile across the barren desert, escorting those who sought to uncover ancient southwestern artifacts and treasures. History books remember him as the man who located the towering Rainbow Bridge.

Louisa's health failed not long after John's death. She and Clyde Coville, a partner in the Kayenta Ranch, sold the property, and Louisa went to live with her son in Skull Valley outside of Prescott. She died on September 18, 1945.

The little girl who once ran in fear from attacking Indians spent her life among the Navajos, traded with them, walked and talked with them, studied their language, their art and their culture, and deeply cared about them for more than fifty years. She is considered one of the first Anglos to understand and preserve the culture of the Navajo people.

"As a guest in a land where most white people are regarded with suspicion," she once said, "always remember that your acceptance by The People will depend on your ability to accept with dignity, sympathy, and honesty the Navajo way of life."

ANOTHER NOTABLE WOMAN

ANNA MAGDALENA BOX NEAL

[1870~1950]

The *Los Angeles Herald* proclaimed Anna Magdalena Box Neal "one of the most charming, genial and appreciative of landladies." The strikingly tall woman made her mark in Oracle, Arizona, in 1895 when she opened the magnificent Mountain View Hotel.

A mixture of Caucasian, African American, and Cherokee, Annie, as she was called, was about nine years old when she arrived in Tucson with her family. She attended St. Joseph's Convent and Academy for Females, run by the Sisters of St. Joseph of Carondelet, during which time she wrote and supposedly published several musical pieces before illness forced her to quit school at age fourteen.

After two failed marriages, Annie wed William "Curly" Neal in 1892. Curly, twenty years older, was considered the wealthiest African American in Tucson. He ran the Tucson-to-Mammoth stage, owned property in Tucson and Oracle, and handled several lucrative delivery contracts.

Curly built the Mountain View in Oracle with Annie serving as its gracious hostess. The two-story adobe structure stood resplendent on 160 acres against the northern slopes of the Santa Catalina Mountains, encircled with verandas and porches that offered cool breezes on hot Arizona nights. Annie offered her guests clean accommodations and savory cuisine, a talent she learned from the Sisters of St. Joseph.

Picnics, dances, and church services kept the Mountain View hopping as the center of community activities. Annie maintained a school for her guests' children and was authorized by the Catholic Church to baptize babies between priests' visits.

Soft-spoken and well educated, Annie was also a crack shot and rode shotgun for Curly on his gold bullion deliveries. She held shooting matches to entertain her guests and once confessed, "the only hotel guest to whom I ever lost a shooting match was [William Frederick "Buffalo Bill"] Cody." Cody owned mines near Oracle and often stayed at the Mountain View.

Annie and Curly were an integral part of Oracle society until the late 1920s, when the nation's rising racial prejudices excluded them from the community. When Annie died in 1950, two old miners were her only guests at the Mountain View.

WESTERN HOSPITALITY

Elizabeth Hudson Smith

[CIRCA 1879–1935]

African American women have been a presence on the western frontier for over three hundred years, sometimes barely visible and rarely with a voice of their own. Initially, many of these women came as chattel of white slaveholders. During the turmoil of the Civil War, both men and women fled their masters, seeking opportunities in the loosely woven fabric of western communities. Few historians have reported the deeds and misdeeds of this feminine minority, yet their contributions to western society were significant.

One of these women was Elizabeth Hudson Smith, who arrived in Wickenburg, Arizona, in August 1897. She and her husband Bill easily blended into the small mining community that already consisted of Mexicans, Indians, Asians, and European-Americans. As the only black couple in town, they were just another pair of adventurers who had braved the Arizona desert to settle in this sparsely populated region. Most came seeking one of the rich veins of gold that had been cropping up since 1863. Elizabeth, however, had her mind set on a more prosperous venture.

Little is known of Elizabeth's childhood. She was probably born in Alabama around 1879. No records exist of her mother, but Sales Hudson, her father, was born into slavery on the Young plantation in Frankfort, Kentucky. After several failed escape attempts, he was sold to the Hudson family. His brother, James Young, successfully escaped. James established a home in Springfield, Illinois, and his family members were Elizabeth's only known relatives. She met Bill Smith, a porter on the Santa Fe, Prescott and Phoenix Railroad, through her uncle James, and the couple married in Chicago on September 28, 1896.

Shortly after their arrival in Wickenburg, Elizabeth and Bill acquired positions at the Baxter Hotel. Bill managed the place and served as bartender, although he often drank more than he sold, while Elizabeth cooked and cleaned. Before long, her reputation as a fine chef brought townspeople into the hotel to taste her delectable meals.

Where Elizabeth acquired her business acumen remains a mystery. The tall, commanding woman was well educated and some believed that she attended

Northwestern University in Evanston, Illinois, but school records do not list her. She spoke fluent French, which led to the belief she may have attended a black college in New Orleans. Again, her name cannot be found as attending any known college that accepted African American women during the late 1800s.

Elizabeth's astute business sense attracted the attention of Santa Fe Railway officials, and they approached her about building a hotel closer to the railway station, allowing passengers to dine and spend the night before continuing their journeys. Bill's mother, Vernetta Smith, had deeded her house in Illinois to her son before her death in 1899. Bill mortgaged the house, and the proceeds probably provided the couple with the capital needed for this expensive undertaking.

Elizabeth hired Phoenix architect James Creighton to design the building that would become the first two-story brick structure in Wickenburg. Twelve-inch-thick walls blocked out the summer sun, while numerous fireplaces kept rooms cozy and warm during the winter months. Six giant chimneys welcomed those entering town, and wood cook stoves heated up the succulent repasts for which Elizabeth had become renowned.

As devout Presbyterians, Elizabeth and James Creighton designed a cross embedded in the lobby floor, welcoming those who stepped across the threshold. Both were co-founders of Wickenburg's Community Church, later known as the First Presbyterian Church.

Opening in September 1905, Elizabeth advertised the Vernetta Hotel, named after Bill's mother, as having "lovely rooms—quiet and well-ventilated." Accommodating about fifty guests, the *Arizona Journal Miner* touted the hotel as "the finest in town."

Railroad officials were delighted with the new Vernetta Hotel. They built a walkway from the train station right to the front door. Passengers had plenty of time to down a drink in the Black and Tan Saloon run by Bill, or to partake of some of Elizabeth's fine dining before continuing their journeys. Those who stayed overnight delighted in the clean rooms and excellent service.

Miners knew they were welcome at the Vernetta, along with more refined folks coming in from big cities. A bank was added to the lobby, along with a post office, a shoeshine stand, and a radio repair shop. The hotel provided a place for civic meetings and local entertainment. By 1909, Elizabeth was bringing in traveling shows, with performances held in the backyard of the hotel until she built an opera house in town. She even did a little acting herself on occasion. An avid bridge player, she invited the townswomen to play cards in the lobby so she could participate whenever her duties allowed. She was always included in social events and family celebrations.

Her charity extended beyond the Vernetta's walls, and she offered a helping hand as well as her pocketbook to anyone in need. More than one miner was grubstaked through Elizabeth's generosity.

As time passed, Bill Smith had less and less to do with the hotel. He disappeared for days, sometimes weeks, bottle in hand, coming home when he ran out of money. Elizabeth grew tired of supporting his liquor habit. On November 22, 1912, she was granted a divorce on the grounds of desertion and abandonment. Bill remained a drifter the rest of his life and died in California in 1926.

By now, Elizabeth's dining and hotel establishment was known far and wide. People drove from Phoenix to partake of her scrumptious feasts and enjoy an evening of entertainment. She brought African American singer Bill Butler from Chicago to entertain her guests and play the grand piano she placed in the hotel lobby. With her knowledge of the French language, she was soon in demand to conduct lessons.

Along with her opera house, Elizabeth acquired a ranch to provide livestock for the hotel's kitchen. She fed her guests vegetables and fruits grown on her farm down by the Hassayampa River, employing Dan Davis, a clubfooted, disheveled, and mentally challenged man, ostracized by the town, to help run the place.

Every child in town knew if they hung out at the back door of the Vernetta, they might walk away with some of Elizabeth's homemade bread or, even better, one of her legendary chocolate chip cookies.

In addition to the hotel, Elizabeth also owned about twelve rental houses, a restaurant, a barbershop, and about ten mining claims in and around Wickenburg. She was a leading figure in the community, and her success contributed to the economic growth of the town.

Yet as racial prejudice permeated into the West, the people of Wickenburg entered the caldron of bigotry that pervaded the country. New hotels sprang up and white travelers avoided the Vernetta. Those who did venture into Elizabeth's establishment assumed she was the hotel maid. Local women no longer met in the lobby to play cards. When they gathered in their homes, they closed their shutters to avoid Elizabeth's questioning looks. She was no longer welcome in the church she had helped establish. Those who had benefitted from her charity offered nothing in return. She became a stranger among old friends.

Elizabeth continued to run the Vernetta, but her health deteriorated. She died March 25, 1935, with her death certificate noting she "should have gone to bed and did not." The next day, the hotel dining room closed its doors forever.

The *Hassayampa Sun* obituary noted her "many deeds of kindness to the community," but the town refused to allow Elizabeth to be buried in the whites-only cemetery. She was buried with the unknown miners, Mexicans, and Chinese in the Garcia Cemetery on the outskirts of town.

Today, the Vernetta Hotel is on the National Register of Historic Buildings. The giant chimneys were destroyed years ago, but the thick brick walls and the cross-designed floor remain as a tribute to the enterprising woman who brought a semblance of cohesiveness to a tiny desert town on the Arizona frontier.

PRINTER'S INK

Angela Hutchinson Hammer

[1870–1952]

Newspaper publishers sometimes go to extreme lengths to get out the news. Few were as determined as Angela Hutchinson Hammer, who set up a print shop in an open corral to publish the *Casa Grande Valley Dispatch*. Angie, as she was called, was already a seasoned publisher and considered this outdoor foray into printing a mere stopgap in her pursuit to bring all the news to the public. Besides, local folks enjoyed watching the old printing press crank out the comings and goings of their neighbors, as well as the latest controversies of ongoing water issues in this central Arizona agricultural valley.

The year 1913 was a hard one for Angie and her three sons, but when the first issue of the *Casa Grande Valley Dispatch* went to press on January 1, 1914, she hoped her troubled times were over.

The second of five daughters born to William and Sarah Hutchinson, Angie arrived on November 30, 1870. Her engineer father built and operated stamp mills in mining communities across the West, never settling in one place for long. In 1881 he headed for work at the Silver King Mine in Arizona, leaving Angie and three of her sisters behind in a Virginia City, Nevada, orphanage until the threat of Indian attacks abated along the untamed frontier.

The Hutchinson family moved to Phoenix in the late 1880s. Teenager Angie found work folding fliers for the *Phoenix Republican* newspaper, and eventually learned to set type. She later graduated from Miss Clara A. Evans' Teacher Training College and acquired her first teaching position with the Wickenburg School District in 1889.

Returning to Phoenix during the summer break, she worked as a composer and chirographer (typographer) for the *Phoenix Evening Gazette*. Printer's ink must have gotten under her nails and "into her blood," as they say, for she decided to forego her teaching position and stay with the paper for a while. She resumed

ANGELA HUTCHINSON HAMMER

teaching in 1892, attaining a post with Enterprise School just north of Gila Bend, but was back in Wickenburg for the following school year.

In 1896 Angie married building contractor Joseph Hammer. Their son Louie was born in 1897, Bill arrived in 1899, and Marvin in 1902. By 1903, however, the marriage was over and she was left with $500 and three young boys to support. She purchased the *Wickenburg Miner* newspaper for $250 and set out to prove she was a newspaperwoman.

Unfortunately, the *Miner*'s printing press dated back to the 1830s, and Angie soon realized the list of advertisers she had purchased, as well as a list of subscribers, contained half-truths and inflated figures. Undaunted, she bartered with advertisers and subscribers, taking fruits and vegetables as payment for ads and copies of the paper.

Slowly, the *Wickenburg Miner* prospered. Angie eventually bought out her competitor, the *News–Herald*.

In 1909 she contracted with the Santa Fe Railway for advertising and printing in return for free train travel. To broaden the scope of her newspaper, she visited small mining communities, each yearning for a newspaper of its own. She arranged to print a front page for these small towns attached to the regular issue of the *Wickenburg Miner*. Her "desert newspaper chain" consisted of the *Eagle's Eye* in Aguila, the *Wenden News*, the *Swansea Times*, and the *Salome Sun*. Each week she made the rounds of the towns, gathering news from local correspondents.

Wickenburg's population hovered just over five hundred about the time the town incorporated in 1909, and the fifteen local saloons did a rollicking business. Angie backed the Women's Christian Temperance Union that encouraged county voters to ban liquor and dry up their towns. Her editorials were so outspoken against saloon owners that fights broke out between her supporters and bar patrons, and she received threats to herself and her press. The town voted the saloonkeepers out, although most just moved across the county line and set up their bars once more.

Politics in Wickenburg got nasty, and Angie was right in the middle of the fray. Fearing for her children's safety, she hired a manager for the *Miner* and moved to Phoenix, setting up Hammer and Sons Print Shop.

In the summer of 1913, Ted Healey, who owned the *Bulletin* in Cochise County, proposed a partnership between himself and Angie to run a newspaper in the small farming community of Casa Grande. Angie admitted she "was so intrigued with the exciting news of settlers swarming in to Casa Grande Valley that it didn't take much persuasion from Ted Healey to induce me to make the move."

Healey had a lot to say but not much money to back a newspaper. Angie and her boys moved their printing equipment to Casa Grande, and on September 11,

1913, the first issue of the Casa Grande *Bulletin* hit the streets. Angie did most of the work while Healey supposedly was busy soliciting business. Angie's money bought the paper stock and supplies, although any profits were split equally between the partners.

At the time, Casa Grande was torn between two factions proposing diverse water remedies for the agricultural area. Angie backed the Casa Grande Water Users Association, which argued for construction of a dam at San Carlos, while. Ted Healey preferred pumping ground water or paying for water provided by canal companies. Each expected to use the *Bulletin* to support their cause, and the partnership fell apart.

When Angie learned Healey planned to abscond with her printing equipment, she and her boys removed the printing press in the dead of night, securing it in a horse barn out of Healey's reach. She left behind the subscription list Healey claimed was worth $15,000 as payment for his half of the business. And so, on that first day of January 1914, the *Casa Grande Valley Dispatch* came to life in the open-air barn.

Healey continued to print the *Bulletin,* and the water war raged between the two newspapers. "We carried on a crossfire of not so friendly words," Angie recalled, "much to the amusement of some of our readers and to the dismay of others... I refrained from calling names or making charges against him, but he continued writing that his equipment had been stolen."

She eventually relocated her printing press in town, but in May 1914, a bakery fire swiftly spread from one wooden building to another, consuming most of Casa Grande's business district. Fortunately, her print shop was spared. Within days, however, her home, about twelve miles from town, burned to the ground. She and her boys moved into their barn until they could rebuild.

In 1917 a local banker offered Angie the chance to buy the *Bulletin,* as Healey was ready to sell. She questioned the banker thoroughly, as he was a friend of Healey's, but quickly recognized "the argument about one good paper in town was so potent that I was quite intrigued. I held my faith that the banker was honest in his intentions." Offering her printing machinery and equipment as collateral, she signed a note to buy the *Bulletin,* then watched helplessly when the economy turned sour during the ravages of World War I. Falling behind on her note, she was soon in default. "One by one, different pieces of machinery were sold or moved to a nearby place with my erstwhile partner in charge." Healey had exacted his revenge.

Although sympathetic, the banker told Angie that women were not cut out for newspaper work. Retaining her subscription list, she tried in vain to keep the *Dispatch* running by having it printed in Phoenix and eventually obtaining a contract to print Eloy's newspaper, the *Cotton City News*. By spring 1918, however, she said farewell to her readers. "It is with a certain degree of regret that I quit the weekly talks and close contact with the *Dispatch* family of subscribers, but I hand over the reins with the hope of serving them and all the people of the County and State in another way, by becoming their representative in the State Legislature." Angie lost her bid to become a legislator.

Meanwhile, her sons Louie and Bill enlisted in the army. The local doctor called on Angie to help treat influenza victims during the 1917–1918 epidemic until she and Marvin, her only child left at home, came down with the virus. Both fully recovered, and Angie was delighted when her two boys returned from the war unscathed.

Two years had passed since she relinquished the reins of the *Casa Grande Valley Dispatch*, with several subsequent owners running it into the ground. She was now selling real estate and making a comfortable living, yet the lure of newspaper ink drew her back, and she took over the failing tabloid in the fall of 1919. Loyal subscribers and advertisers welcomed her return, and the business flourished.

Angie backed James M. Cox as the U.S. presidential candidate in 1920. When he lost by a landslide to Republican Warren G. Harding, she suddenly found herself losing government printing contracts, as did most Democratic newspapers. She served as a delegate to the Democratic conference in Tucson in May 1922, but by the following March she had severed her newspaper ties with the Democratic Party to become an independent publication. The next year the *Arizona Gazette* lauded the *Dispatch* as "one of the most alert and readable of our contemporaries."

Angie sold the *Dispatch* in late 1924, telling her readers she had "enjoyed the work even though it took me through troubled times and to the threshold of disaster." And although she had seen her fiftieth birthday several years before, she was not yet ready to sit back and relax.

Offered the opportunity to buy the struggling *Messenger* newspaper in Phoenix, she established the Messenger Printing Company and went into the venture with sons Bill and Marvin. Turning a profit, she took the paper from a weekly to a daily and changed the name to the *Arizona Messenger* and later the *Bee-Messenger*.

Bad economic times sent the paper spiraling downward as the Great Depression took hold across the nation. The *Bee-Messenger* faltered after only six months. In 1932 Angie returned to publishing the weekly *Arizona Messenger*, also printing the *Phoenix Shopping News* for a short time.

With Bill and Marvin firmly established in the newspaper business, Angie turned her attention to civic duties. She had served as immigration commissioner for Pinal County since 1915, promoting Arizona tourism through her newspaper. She sat on the Arizona State Board of Social Security and Welfare from 1938 until 1943. She was also active in the Phoenix Business and Professional Women's Association, the Phoenix Pen Women's Association, and the Phoenix Writers Club, although she confessed her "happiest days were spent in the middle of a hot controversy as editor of a local newspaper."

Her oldest son Louie lost his wife in 1938 and needed help with his two small children. Angie sold her interest in the *Arizona Messenger,* turned over the Messenger Printing Company to Bill and Marvin, and returned to Casa Grande to tend to her grandchildren. She returned to Wickenburg in her later years and died in Phoenix on April 9, 1952.

In 1965 Angela Hutchinson Hammer was the first women elected to the Arizona Newspaper Association's Hall of Fame. She was "born with a terrific zest for living and love for her fellowman," said one observer, "ever ready to pick up the cause for the side she believed to be right… She was the embodiment of the pioneer woman."

WOMEN WHO EDUCATED

Education in Arizona has come a long way from the one-room dirt floor schoolhouses once scattered across the western frontier. Some of the first schools were set up in tents, old saloons, jailhouses, and abandoned miners' cabins to accommodate the ever-increasing number of children who often journeyed miles to the nearest school. If the classroom had anything at all that served as desks, they might be upturned packing crates or planks full of splinters. One teacher used an old flour barrel, turned upside down, as her desk. Blackboards did not exist. Lessons were often written on a couple of boards nailed together and painted black. With chalk hard to come by, talc from nearby mines was often used to write lessons on the board. Water had to be hauled from the nearest watering hole.

The first Prescott teacher was paid with fees acquired from taxing saloons and gambling establishments. And although women made up the bulk of teachers in the Old West, they were paid far less than their male counterparts and had to leave their positions if they chose to marry.

When Mary Elizabeth Post arrived in Ehrenberg, she was assigned an abandoned saloon in which to conduct classes. Relocating to Yuma, her schoolhouse was an old jail.

Hopi teacher Polingaysi Qöyawayma (Elizabeth White) straddled two worlds as she attempted to bridge the gap between Anglo and Hopi cultures. Eulalia "Sister" Bourne taught English to her mainly Spanish-speaking students by having them write and publish a newsletter detailing their everyday lives.

Maria Urquides' Hispanic background made her the ideal teacher for bilingual Tucson schools, although she readily admitted she might go to hell after following orders to punish students for speaking Spanish in the classroom.

African American Rebecca Dallis had an enormous effect on the black children of Casa Grande even though she earned less than Anglo teachers, and her school survived on fewer funds than those of the nearby white school.

So many Arizona women made their mark in education yet remain unrecognized and unrewarded. They did not teach for the money or fame. They had a driving need to improve the lives of Arizona's children, and by doing so they contributed to the betterment of entire communities.

TEACHING IN THE GLORY HOLE

Mary Elizabeth Post

[1841–1934]

According to Mary Elizabeth Post, who arrived in Arizona Territory in 1872, "[T]he country around Yuma was known in the mining world as the 'gloryhole' [*sic*] section of the Southwest, and the town was continually being stirred up with stories of 'rich finds.' " One of Yuma's most lucrative discoveries, however, was that of the petite young woman who came to teach the children of Yuma, many of whom could not speak English.

Only the fifth female schoolteacher in the territory, Mary crossed the desert from San Diego in a "mud wagon" and landed on the shores of the Colorado River on April 13, 1872. She had been teaching since the age of fifteen, but had never experienced such rough and crude surroundings as those that greeted her in Arizona City (renamed Yuma in 1873).

Her early years were spent in Elizabethtown, New York, where she was born on June 17, 1841, the oldest of nine children. In 1856 she acquired her first teaching job while continuing her own education. Denied entrance into the University of Vermont, which did not yet admit women, she attended and graduated from the Burlington (Vermont) Female Seminary in 1863. Later that year the family moved to Iowa, where Mary acquired a position with Allamakee College and Normal School in the far northeastern part of the state. She remained there for five years.

After breaking her engagement to a young man, she took a position in Lansing, Iowa. A visit with an uncle in California changed her life.

Mary left by train for San Francisco in January 1872. From there she took a steamer to San Diego, a three-day passage. Her plans were to establish a girls' school, but she soon realized the population of San Diego, hovering around 2,300, did not yet warrant such a venture.

About this time, the territory of Arizona sent out a call for teachers. Mary booked passage on the next stagecoach heading east, picked out her thinnest dresses, purchased a broad-brimmed hat to ward off Arizona's extreme temperatures, and bought a lightweight suitcase—she was allowed only thirty pounds of baggage.

According to Mary, "The vehicle in which the trip was made was not a Concord stage, such as was afterwards put upon the line, but what was known in common parlance as a 'mud-wagon.' It had two seats, and could carry three persons besides the driver, was covered with canvas as a protection against the sun, with curtains on the sides which could be raised or lowered at pleasure." Because the stage was full, "there was nothing to do but sit erect in that stage for forty-eight hours, the only respite being the short stops made three times each day for meals."

Mary was not used to fixins' of beans, bacon, and strong black coffee, but she learned to enjoy "Arizona strawberries," pink kidney beans that were a mainstay throughout the West.

Arriving in Yuma, she spent ten days waiting for a steamer to take her one hundred miles upriver to her first teaching post in Ehrenberg. She found herself a rarity, as few white women lived in town. "The ten days spent in Yuma, waiting for the steamer passed very pleasantly," she recalled, "but during that time I never stepped into the street alone, not that it was really dangerous to do so, but the amount of attention attracted made it more comfortable to have a companion."

The steamer took five days to reach Ehrenberg, including several hours stranded on a sandbar. She lost her hat overboard, encountered Native Americans who supplied wood to fuel the ship, and was appalled when the captain pulled out his whiskey flask in her presence.

The town of Ehrenberg was booming in the early 1870s. Freight for mining communities and the military came through the river port that was home to about five hundred individuals. Mary rented a room in one of the small adobe houses and attempted to converse with her Spanish-speaking landlady.

The language barrier worsened when she began teaching, as none of her fifteen students spoke English. She relied temporarily on a translator, but since she was already proficient in French and Latin, she quickly learned the Spanish language.

The Ehrenberg School, probably the third public school in Arizona Territory, was housed in an old saloon, and occasionally a thirsty former patron staggered into the classroom. Most made a hasty retreat, but some lingered and listened for a while.

Mary taught in Ehrenberg for five months before accepting a position in Yuma, a predominantly Spanish-speaking community. The steamer trip back down the Colorado River was much more pleasant than the one she had endured a few months earlier.

Insisting her Yuma students attend regularly, something they were not used to doing, the new schoolteacher often had to go after her truant charges, much to the disgruntlement of their parents, who saw no reason for daily lessons.

Determined to improve her relationships with these families, Mary ordered an array of patterns and spent hours teaching mothers how to sew clothing for their children. She and her pupils, along with their families, soon reached an accord on school participation.

Yet prim and proper Mary was unprepared for the lawlessness that permeated Yuma's streets. When the first legal hanging in Arizona Territory was held in town, she refused to hold class that day. Uneasy about the violence and turmoil, she accepted a position as vice principal of a San Diego school for the following year.

The Yuma Board of Trustees initiated vast improvements in the public school system and invited Mary back to take charge. She accepted the challenge, particularly when they proposed a separation of girls and boys in the classroom. She persuaded her brother, Albert Post, to come west and teach the boys while she managed the girls. A musician, Albert brought the first organ to Yuma.

The school was housed in the old courthouse and jail. According to Mary, "the walls were still ornamented with the scrawls, covered though not hidden by whitewash with which the former occupants had whiled away their time."

In addition to poor housing, supplies were lacking as well. The brother and sister team worked together on fundraisers for school materials, particularly books. One horse race netted $600, and at Christmastime, with the help of townspeople, they purchased toys for the children and decorated one of the town's first Christmas trees. Albert coached the students in a Christmas musical while Mary helped sew dresses for the girls and shirts for the boys. "I doubt if there was a better dressed company of children in all the land," she proudly boasted.

Mexican women were eager to learn American cooking, and Mary gladly provided instructions. A bounty of cakes came out of the ovens that winter.

By now she had endeared herself to the town, becoming an integral part of the lives of her pupils and their families. She was invited to baptisms and first communions, attended family celebrations, and endured heartrending tragedies.

MARY ELIZABETH POST

She felt the town had become civilized until Yuma Territorial Prison was completed in 1877. And although she feared the presence of prisoners would bring undesirable elements to Yuma, encouraging the community to revert to its bawdy and dangerous origins, she also provided occupational therapy for some of the women inmates.

After Albert Post married, Mary reveled in the addition of nieces and nephews to entertain and educate. In particular, Albert's oldest daughter, also named Mary, was a favorite of her Aunt Mary. As other children came along, Mary asked to take the little girl to live with her, but the child's parents refused. Albert died in 1886, leaving a widow and three children. His wife, overwhelmed with the sole care of her family, allowed her sister-in-law to take young Mary on a temporary basis. Within the month, however, the child died after her dress caught fire and she succumbed to her injuries. Mary was devastated. She had considered little Mary almost her own.

Always fretting over the lack of style in Yuma, Mary spent a summer in San Diego purchasing hats, materials, and all the trimmings. Upon her return, she opened a millinery shop in one room of her house. Yet by the following spring, she had to close the doors on her small enterprise as it took too much time away from her students.

Challenged for her job by a man who felt the school should hire only male educators and not female teachers sympathizing with the Mexican populace, Mary set out to prove him wrong. Her competitor persuaded women who had never voted in a school board election to mark their ballots for his slate of candidates, even handing them slips of paper containing the names of those who agreed with his position. On election day, Mary rode out to the Mexican neighborhoods she knew so well and escorted the mothers of her students to the polls, providing them with her own slate of candidates and instructing the women to be very careful to spell the names correctly. "To these women," said one friend, "it was the most perfectly natural thing in the world that this person who had been teaching Americanism in many forms should take them to the polls for the first time." She easily retained her position.

Now past sixty years old, Mary spent less time at school, but continued to tutor children outside the classroom. She also became a force behind local women's organizations as a delegate to annual conventions of the Arizona Federation of Women's Clubs and an avid supporter of the women's suffrage movement.

Mary retired from teaching about the time Arizona passed its first pension law in 1912, and became the first recipient of the state teachers' retirement fund, garnering $50 a month. She continued to work by interpreting for the

Reclamation Service, the courts, and Catholic priests. For a while she even went door-to-door selling corsets.

One of her first acquisitions after retiring was a complete riding outfit—jacket, shirtwaist, divided skirt, hat, boots, and gloves. She added one of the latest saddles, climbed aboard her newly purchased horse, and rode out of town, much to the delight and astonishment of townsfolk.

Mary had been raised in the Methodist Church, but in early Yuma the only house of worship was a small adobe Catholic church that she supported for years. When a Methodist church was built, she attended and taught Sunday school, but continued to be a presence in the Catholic congregation that had welcomed her years before. In 1915, at the age of seventy-four, she joined the Catholic faith.

Arizona did not forget Mary after she retired. In 1918 the University of Arizona awarded her an honorary Master of Arts degree for her humanitarian work in predominately Spanish-speaking communities. Two years later, she helped open the first public library in Yuma, serving on the library board until her death.

In an interview during her eighty-sixth year, she was asked why she never married. "It was not for lack of opportunity," she said, "but I was in love with my work. I think I was born to be a teacher." And she could still turn heads. A local fireman confessed during this time, "Just between you and me, she is better company than half the girls I have for partners at our dances."

On September 15, 1934, ninety-three-year-old Mary Elizabeth Post died. Her body lay in state for twenty-four hours, allowing the people of Yuma to pay their respects. Protestants and Catholics alike attended her wake. The evening before her funeral, a radio memorial service aired in her honor.

Mary witnessed the arrival of the railroad in Yuma, as well as telephones, automobiles, and electric lights. She was probably a little embarrassed when ladies' hemlines crept above the knees and couples held hands in public. Yet nothing stopped her from teaching the children of Yuma, not the language barrier nor the opinions of those who believed women should stay at home and let men run the schools. Yuma citizens knew they had struck it rich when this petite young woman rode into town and decided to stay and teach for the next fifty years.

FROM THE FAMILIAR
TO THE UNKNOWN

Polingaysi Qöyawayma (Elizabeth White)

[1892–1990]

Most of her life, Polingaysi Qöyawayma walked between two different worlds: The community of her birth in 1892 on Third Mesa of the Hopi community in northern Arizona, and the white society she chose to enter at a very early age. As a teacher, she combined these factions by educating both cultures about the differences that made them distinctive and the similarities they shared.

Born in Oraibi, considered the oldest continuously inhabited community in the United States, Polingaysi displayed an intense inquisitiveness about the world around her. When the U.S. government opened a school at the base of the mesa and insisted all Hopi children attend, her mother hid her so school authorities would not take her. But Polingaysi's curiosity soon led her down the trail and into the schoolhouse.

It did not take long for someone to notice the dirty little girl. She was scrubbed clean and given new clothes to wear. As she and the rest of the students sat in the classroom, they had no idea what the teacher was saying, but they dutifully copied the strange marks he made on the blackboard.

That evening when her mother asked who had taken her to the school, Polingaysi confessed she had gone willingly. "You have taken a step in the wrong direction," her mother cried. "A step away from your Hopi people. You have brought grief to us. To me, to your father and to your grandparents. Now you must continue to go to school each day. You have brought this thing upon yourself, and there is no turning back."

Polingaysi was given the name "Bessie" by the new schoolteacher, as he found most Hopi names too difficult to pronounce. She enjoyed going to school, wearing the soft clothing, and eating the abundance of food she was offered. She found her adventure into the white world exciting and enticing. Besides, her Oraibi community was in the throes of intense discord.

In September 1906 disagreements within Oraibi pitted one Hopi family against another. Among the issues that separated the community was whether the children should attend the government school. Those who accepted the invasion of white school authorities into their children's lives demanded that those who refused to send their children to the government-run school leave the village. To avoid the conflict, Polingaysi's father built a new home for his family below the mesa at Kiakotsmovi—New Oraibi.

That same fall, Polingaysi heard of a school in Riverside, California, that educated Indians from many tribes. Her parents realized they could not contain their daughter's strong will and reluctantly allowed her to go.

Sherman Institute opened Polingaysi's eyes to new surroundings and a wealth of learning. She still knew little English, but her strong singing voice soon attracted attention and she was given the lead in a school play. She also learned to sew, making her own clothes and charging others for her services. She liked having her own money.

Spending four years at Sherman, she studied hard and became proficient in the English language. Her Hopi name translates to "Butterfly Sitting among the Flowers in the Breeze," yet Polingaysi was never content to just watch the world revolve around her. She embraced the Christian faith and decided to become a missionary.

Returning to her family in 1910, she found readjusting to the Hopi lifestyle difficult. She and her mother clashed over her new American ways, her cooking expertise with store-bought pots and pans, her insistence on a table on which to eat and a soft bed instead of a blanket on the floor. Finally, her father suggested that she go live with the Mennonite family of Reverend Jacob Frey at Moenkopi, forty miles away. Not wanting to sever all ties with his daughter, he gave her a plot of land in New Oraibi on which to build her own house one day. Polingaysi continued her missionary studies under Reverend Frey's tutelage and adopted the name Elizabeth Ruth, which she retained the rest of her life.

Reverend Frey took her to Newton, Kansas, so she could learn typesetting as a profession, and to visit the Mennonite school Bethel Academy (now known as Bethel College). As eager as she was to explore new territory, she was not prepared for the strange looks her brown skin evoked on the streets of Kansas. When a waitress refused to serve her, believing she was of African descent, Polingaysi left in tears. "What can one do about one's skin?" she said. "We, who are clay blended by the Master Potter, come from the kiln of Creation in many hues. How can people say one skin is colored, when each has its own coloration? What should it matter that one bowl is dark and other pale, if each is of good design and serves its purpose well?"

In 1911 Polingaysi entered Bethel Academy as Elizabeth Ruth Qöyawayma. Along with her missionary studies she took vocal and piano lessons, all the while working in the school kitchen to pay her tuition. She returned to her family each summer, but found she was growing further away from the Hopi culture.

POLINGAYSI QÖYAWAYMA (ELIZABETH WHITE)

In 1914 twenty-two-year-old Elizabeth returned to Oraibi to begin her missionary work, but she was not very good at recruiting Hopis to the Christian faith. When presented the opportunity to assist a teacher at the Kayenta Indian boarding school, a trading center near the Utah border, she accepted the challenge.

She never had the chance to start her new career; an influenza outbreak in Tuba City closed the school. Helping to nurse the sick, she was soon one of the patients. After recovering, she accepted a job as substitute teacher for Navajo students at the Tuba City boarding school.

Elizabeth had never considered a teaching career, but she discovered that students responded favorably to her educational techniques. Relating their lessons to everyday experiences afforded the children an opportunity to learn the English language, reading, mathematics, and science on their own terms.

Still determined to become a missionary, she entered Los Angeles Bible Institute, returning to Hopi land in 1924 to work as housekeeper in the Hotevilla School. She passed the Indian Service test, qualifying her as an employee of the U.S. government. She was soon asked to take over a classroom.

Forbidden to speak the Hopi language to her students and instructed to tell only American stories, Elizabeth realized the children would not respond to lessons they did not understand. Ignoring the instructions of her superiors, she sang songs and recited familiar Hopi stories in the English language. The children quickly picked up the words as they sang along. When parents complained they wanted their children to learn American ways, she pointed out that teaching from the familiar to the unknown gave the students an understanding in all aspects of education.

During this time, she started building a house in Oraibi on the land her father had given her, laying the foundation and acquiring wood from an old building for the frame. She even bought a piano for her new home.

From Hotevilla, Elizabeth was transferred to Chinle on the Navajo Reservation, then to a Navajo school in Toadlena, New Mexico. She found the Navajo children just as eager to learn when she applied her methods of teaching English using stories they had known all their lives.

At almost forty years old, Elizabeth fell in love. Lloyd White was part Cherokee and did not object to her teaching as did most Hopi men, who wanted stay-at-home wives. They married in 1931 at the Bloomfield Trading Post near Toadlena. When school closed at the end of the year, she took him to Oraibi to meet her parents and to the house she had built. That fall she began teaching at Polacca at the base of First Mesa.

As happy as she was to be back among her people, her marriage faltered. She divorced during her two years at Polacca, then transferred to the school at New Oraibi.

Over the years, Elizabeth had received numerous visitors to her classrooms who were interested in her teaching methods of utilizing the familiar to understand the unknown. "In the fall," she said,

> we use harvest ideas. One day we may have a watermelon party. We sketch the melon, then divide it and eat it. We write descriptive words about it— smooth, round, green, cool, sweet, perhaps. We count the seeds in each portion of melon. We list the uses for the seeds. They can be parched and eaten. They can be used to oil the *piki* stone, and so on.
>
> We talk about home life. We take the child's own home experience as a basis and use it to teach him about the larger community life, and we go on from there to teach him about the state, nation, and world. In that way he becomes aware of his relation to life and his responsibility as an individual.

Her visitors spread Elizabeth's teaching methods beyond Arizona's borders. In 1941 she presented her educational ideas in Chemawa, Oregon, at a summer session of supervisors and teachers from across the United States and Alaska. Upon her return, she received an invitation for her twenty-six-member primary rhythm band to play at the Arizona State Teachers College in Flagstaff, more than one hundred miles from the Hopi Reservation. The children were eager but apprehensive to travel so far from home. As they pulled into town, one of the little girls whispered in Elizabeth's ear, "I'm not afraid of white people." The show was a huge success.

Teaching for more than three decades, Elizabeth retired in 1954. That June she was awarded a bronze medal of commendation and an honor award from the U.S. Department of the Interior for her dedication to the education of Hopi and Navajo children. Because "every deserving young person should have a chance to prove himself," she initiated a scholarship fund for Hopi students to attend Northern Arizona University (formerly Northern Arizona State Teachers College).

Elizabeth wrote her autobiography, *No Turning Back*, in 1964, chronicling her lifelong struggle to live peacefully with her Hopi heritage while working in the white world.

She began experimenting with clay, embedding distinct raised symbols such as ears of corn and Kokopelli figures in her unique pottery. She planned to do more with her music and wanted to translate some of the ancient Hopi songs. But all of her ideas literally went up in smoke in 1974, when her house in New Oraibi burned to the ground. It took her two years to rebuild.

In 1976 the Museum of Northern Arizona unveiled a bronze sculpture of Elizabeth. She received the Arizona Indian Living Treasure Tribute in 1978, along with the Heard Museum's Gold Medal. Bethel Academy recognized her as one of its Outstanding Alumna in 1979.

Back in 1941 Elizabeth wrote a children's story, *The Sun Girl: A True Story about Dawamana, the Little Hopi Indian Maid of Old Oraibi in Arizona and of How She Learned to Dance the Butterfly Dance at Moencopi.* Republished in 1978 by the Museum of Northern Arizona, the book was selected as one of the best books of 1989 by the Arizona State Library Arizona Author Association.

After suffering a stroke in 1981, her health deteriorated, and Elizabeth was finally forced to move out of her home. Polingaysi Qöyawayma died in Phoenix on December 6, 1990, at age ninety-eight.

"Evaluate the best there is in your own culture and hang onto it," she told her students, "for it will always be foremost in your life; but do not fail to take also the best from other cultures to blend with what you already have." She advised not to "set limitations on yourself. If you want more and still more education, reach out for it without fear. You have in you the qualities of persistence and endurance. Use them."

FADED LEVI'S AND BRIGHT RED LIPSTICK

Eulalia "Sister" Collins Bourne

[CIRCA 1892–1984]

With only three years of formal classroom education, Eulalia "Sister" Bourne wanted to teach. "I had no college degree, no high school diploma, no elementary school certificate," she lamented, but her determination won her a position as schoolmarm in Beaver Creek, Arizona, in 1914. Situated in the Verde Valley east of the thriving town of Prescott, Beaver Creek boasted a student population of ten. With the grand salary of $80 a month and the country on the brink of World War I, Eulalia divorced her husband, a man more than twice her age, and struck out on her own. Over the next forty years, she became one of Arizona's most beloved teachers, responsible for the educational needs of children in small remote towns and villages scattered among Arizona's stark, barren mining and ranching communities.

Eulalia Collins was born in Texas around 1892 and raised in the White Mountains of New Mexico. Called "Sister" by a younger sibling who could not pronounce Eulalia, she grew to prefer the nomenclature to her given name. At age sixteen, she married prospector William S. Bourne, and the couple settled in Humbug, Arizona, a small gold-mining community. The marriage only lasted a few years, leaving Sister with no means of support.

When she learned a teacher was needed in the nearby community of Beaver Creek, she spent the summer reading borrowed textbooks in preparation for acquiring a teaching certificate. "The day before the tests I walked nine miles to Castle Hot Springs, took the stage to Congress Junction, and from there the train to Phoenix. My ten dollars had to cover round-trip fare, two nights in a hotel, and incidentals, including food." Existing on donuts, she passed the test, although she almost failed the arithmetic portion.

The ten students at Beaver Creek ranged from ages ten to sixteen. Sister learned how to teach that first year as her pupils flourished. When she was invited back for the 1915–1916 semester, she found over twenty students in her classroom.

Her social life also prospered. However, when gossip spread that she had been seen dancing the one-step to the new and vulgar ragtime music, she was dismissed as an unfit teacher.

Helvetia, a mining camp at the foothills of the Santa Rita Mountains, needed an instructor. Sister discovered the children came mainly from Mexican families, with only a few speaking English. "They had a rule in Arizona at the time," she recalled. "No Spanish on the school grounds. Not a word. I thought that was the silliest thing I ever heard. I determined that if I was to teach them, I had to be able to talk to them." She bought a Spanish grammar book and asked her students to help her learn their language. "They told me about a hundred words and how they laughed when I missed one… It was wonderful."

During her four years at Helvetia, Sister reported that she married Irishman Ernest O'Daugherty, even though he was ill with tuberculosis. Both knew his time was limited, but they were determined to enjoy their remaining days together. Ernest died in December 1919.

Still teaching on the certificate she had acquired six years before, she enrolled at the University of Arizona while teaching in a multilingual Tucson school. "I soon had my doubts about city teaching. It seemed to me there was little chance to use initiative or past experience. In class routines, all the ways and means and devices I had learned or initiated while working with my country pupils counted for nothing." She declared the ten years she spent in Tucson "the saddest, loneliest years I have known."

EULALIA "SISTER" COLLINS BOURNE

Sister supposedly married again while in Tucson, but admitted the union was doomed from the start. Graduating summa cum laude in 1930 with majors in English and Spanish, she happily left town for Redington School in the San Pedro Valley.

Donning a new blue dress, her usual attire for the first day of school, bright red lipstick in place, and hair neatly curled, Sister faced the ten eager faces before her. The children were from Mexican and Mormon ranch families. "The thing I remember most about our school was happiness. We had fun... We were teaching and learning. I showed the kids how to learn, and they showed me how to teach. At Redington, I really became a teacher."

With such eager and ingenious students, Sister looked for opportunities to engage and expand their creative talents. She encouraged her charges to write about their lives on the family ranch and activities within their small community. These stories became the first issues of the school newspaper, *Little Cowpuncher*. The paper contained a story or drawing from every student. First graders dictated their narratives to older children, with everyone learning valuable lessons as they worked together to "get out the news." For more than ten years, wherever Sister taught, the *Little Cowpuncher* appeared in the classroom.

"The little 'magazine' is not intended, as anybody can see, to afford journalistic training," according to Sister. "Even providing language exercises is secondary. The high aim is literature—an attempt to hold the mirror up to life as we live it here, a record of what happens to us—something we can smile over nostalgically in years to come. Of course I want its influence to play a vital part educationally—that is, to being some of the big world...over the mountains into this makeshift schoolroom."

After two years at Redington, Sister filed a claim on one of the last grazing homesteads in Peppersauce Canyon on the north side of the Catalina Mountains. She built an adobe house and ran about fifty head of cattle on her spread. Every Friday she left the Redington School and headed up the road to tend to her ranch. And every Monday morning she raced back down the road to get to school on time. Out of necessity she was soon wearing utilitarian Levi's in the classroom instead of more feminine attire, much to the dismay of school authorities. But she never gave up the bright red lipstick.

In 1935 she accepted a teaching position at Baboquívari on the Poza Nuevo Ranch in Altar Valley, twenty miles from the Mexican border. Of the twenty-eight children at Baboquívari, only a handful spoke English. Utilizing the *Little Cowpuncher* as a teaching tool, her students soon became known for their creative tales. The first issue contained an explanation, written by one of the children, of the publication. "This little paper is written once a month by the Baboquívari

School. We call it 'Little Cowpuncher' because we all live on ranches including our teacher, and we are all born of cowboys. It is written by Baboquívari Mexican boys and girls and that is why the English is so original."

Baboquívari students gained a modicum of fame with their distinctive and often humorous stories. They were invited to sing on the radio and participate in Tucson's rodeo parades, although Sister detested the rodeo experience because of its cruelty to animals. "Regretting all the mistakes as a teacher I made in my lifetime," she once said, "I am most sorry for taking my children to the rodeos. Oh, it was fun and excitement, and they learned a lot. But it was wrong. It is activity based on man's ancient instinct to be brutal to living creatures in his power."

By the time the Baboquívari School was moved to the Espinosa Ranch in 1937, over two hundred copies of *Little Cowpuncher* were spewing off an old mimeograph machine, gaining distribution across the state, even out of the country. Two years later, the school moved again, to the Palo Alto Ranch.

In the fall of 1939 Sister was needed to teach about twenty students at the Sasco Ranch school, about thirty-five miles north of Tucson. There was little money to spend on building maintenance, so Sister painted the school herself, including the blackboards. Startling even the children in her Western attire, her students soon adopted the same clothing style, much to her delight.

After about a year, she moved to the San Fernando School, built on a hill near the Mexican border, the largest in her repertoire of rural learning institutions.

From there she went to Sopori School, about forty-five miles south of Tucson. Still publishing *Little Cowpuncher*, her students eagerly anticipated riding in Tucson's rodeo parade. As the children waited to board the float, a team of runaway horses almost trampled one of the girls. That was the last time she allowed her charges to ride in the parade. Sopori was also the last school to write and publish *Little Cowpuncher*. The newsletter was recognized in 1941 with a Blue Ribbon Award from the Columbia Scholastic Press Association.

In 1951 Sister traded her Peppersauce ranch for property in the foothills of the Galiuro Mountains near the town of Mammoth. Carrying the burden of managing the property and all the incidentals that go along with ranching, such as roping and branding, she sustained broken arms, ribs, hip, pelvis, and a dislocated kidney. When she left Sopori in 1957, she planned to make a living from her ranch, but agreed to substitute teach as long as her well-worn Levi's and dusty boots were acceptable in the classroom.

Before long she was ensconced in a small school in Sierrita, about forty miles of dirt road south of Tucson. Several teachers had come and gone over the last few years, and the twenty students were behind in their schoolwork. What started as a temporary position turned into an eight-year project. She lived in a small shed behind the school and made the one-hundred-mile trip to her homestead every weekend.

Sister did not institute the *Little Cowpuncher* at Sierrita, as it demanded a great deal of time and these children needed to concentrate on their studies. In addition, all of her pupils were Anglo, and the impetus behind the *Cowpuncher* newsletters was Spanish-speaking children writing stories in English.

Yet the Sierrita children held a special place in Sister's heart. Few had ever been off the family ranch. She brought a radio to school so they could listen to the opening of Congress, the inauguration of a president, even the World Series. Thursday-morning broadcasts of the "Standard School Broadcast Music Hour" were a delight for both pupils and teacher, as Sister was a firm believer that music should be part of every school curriculum.

She also believed children should be paid for attending school because "school is work...everyone should be paid for his work."

Friday afternoons might find several of her students in the back seat of her car on their way to her ranch for the weekend. A stopover in Tucson meant a treat of hamburgers and milkshakes, a menu few of the children had ever experienced.

Sister finally retired for good in 1965. She wrote her memoirs about the schools and the children who had influenced her life, barely realizing how much she had given to these rural students in return. *Woman in Levi's* was published in 1967, followed in 1968 by *Nine Months is a Year at Baboquivari School. Ranch Schoolteacher* came out in 1974. Her one children's book, *The Blue Colt,* was published in 1979. She donated all the royalties from her books to the Eulalia "Sister" Bourne Scholarship Fund for students pursuing a career in creative writing at the University of Arizona.

In 1973 Sister was named Woman of the Year by the Arizona Press Women organization. She received the Distinguished Citizen Award from the University of Arizona Alumni Association in 1975 and the university's Service Recognition Award the following year. The Arizona State Library Association named her Arizona's Outstanding Author in 1983.

Eulalia "Sister" Bourne died on May 1, 1984, at her ranch in the Galiuro Mountains. She was posthumously inducted into the Cowgirl Hall of Fame in 1996. She once confessed, "I supposed other teachers all knew much more than I did. My work was tentatively hacking my way through the forest of ignorance (especially my own)."

BEHIND THE SHEET

Rebecca Huey Dallis
[1896–1971]

School segregation existed in Arizona schools almost from the onset, when Mexican children were refused an education in many predominantly white communities. As African Americans migrated west after the Civil War, laws banishing them from the schoolroom started appearing on legislative books. A 1909 Arizona law allowed segregation of black students, and in 1912 segregation was ordered in all grade schools. By 1921 the legislation included high schools, making Arizona one of the strictest western states to ban blacks from white classrooms.

Many small towns with just a few black pupils could not afford to build a second school and instituted a unique method of separation by hanging a bed sheet between the races. While teachers usually taught all the children together, they sent black students behind the sheet when school officials arrived for a visit. This was the atmosphere that African American Rebecca Huey Dallis encountered when she came to Arizona to teach in 1929.

Born in Connersville, Indiana, in 1896, Rebecca graduated from Swift Memorial College in Rogersville, Tennessee, in 1924. Reverend William Henderson Franklin, the son of slave parents, had established Swift in 1883, opening the world of education to southern African American students.

Rebecca married William Curtis Dallis on December 23, 1923, and received her teaching certificate the following year. The couple moved to Phoenix in 1929. William opened the Dallis Funeral Home, which he operated until 1932. Rebecca reportedly taught school in Mobile, Arizona, a predominantly black community about thirty miles southwest of Phoenix, from 1932 until 1939. At the time, two railroad cars served as segregated schoolhouses for black and white students.

She earned her master of arts in education from the University of Arizona in 1935. Four years later she and William moved to Casa Grande.

In 1933 the black population of Casa Grande had increased to the point that a separate "colored school" was "required by the laws of the state," according to the *Casa Grande Dispatch*. In September 1939 Rebecca replaced the retiring teacher at the one-room Southside Colored Grammar School, located in a far corner on the grounds of the white South School. The long narrow building accommodated between fifty and seventy students under Rebecca's tutelage. As one student remembered, entering the long narrow school building made her feel "like cattle through a chute."

"You had to listen to all the noise from everybody," recalled another student. "There were no divisions or separation in that building… You had a little huddle over there being taught and you had to listen to all that noise…but we did the best we could because that's all we had."

Earning about one-third less than her white counterparts, Rebecca was allotted tattered textbooks with missing pages and secondhand, worn-out chalk from nearby South School. She worked without benefit of a library or any science equipment. Her students, forbidden to ride the school buses with white students and banned from school playgrounds when white children were at recess, played with often-deflated soccer balls and old baseballs and bats. "We never got any new nothin'," said one of her students.

Yet Rebecca was determined to produce strong, educated students. Her courses of study consisted of extracurricular subjects as well as academic classes. She had older children tutor youngsters outside under a tree to reduce the noise in the cramped classroom. When she discovered some of her students needed an understanding of Spanish to enroll in college, she ordered a correspondence course and learned the language right along with them. Many of her students went on to higher education. "She expected all of us to go to college," one of her students recalled.

When her pupils performed in a musical program for the Parent Teachers Association in 1942, she provided the children with their "most popular medium of expression. Negro folk music is a part of the historical background of the nation," she wrote in 1935, "and indeed, is one of the types of real American folk music."

With no school facilities for classes such as home economics, she taught students how to cook in her own kitchen. Knowing that "the home environment among negroes in some sections is not satisfactory this type of training is highly desirable…"

William Dallis also taught some of the students, concentrating on high school subjects, except for algebra, which apparently was Rebecca's realm of expertise. He also used a room in their house or their screened porch to alleviate overcrowding at the school.

Integration became a volatile subject in Casa Grande during the late 1940s, when a white farmwoman, Louise Henness, convinced the board of education to approve equal schooling for all the town's children. However, public opinion vetoed the vote for integration. Two years later, Henness again opened the

REBECCA HUEY DALLIS

discussion of integration, and the Casa Grande High School Board approved the issue. (Arizona did not endorse statewide integration until 1953.)

During this time, Rebecca worked diligently with the school board to improve conditions at Southside Colored Grammar School. "The school is a huge factory preparing individuals for the business of life," she wrote. "The success of the factory depends entirely on the type of product it turns out and the fitness of the product for its particular work in the world of vocations and avocations. The youth who leaves the factory unfitted for work and play is a concrete demonstration of the inefficiency of the factory."

In 1952 she left the narrow classroom of Southside to teach at Casa Grande's new East School, acquiring the title of head teacher. But not until 1960 did the school board feel comfortable naming her principal, a job she had performed for the last eight years. Along with her principal duties, she worked with developmentally challenged children at East School, utilizing methods she had learned while taking post-graduate classes at Arizona State University and the University of Southern California.

Rebecca retired from East School in 1962, but she certainly did not retire from teaching. Students came to her house to take piano lessons, and she was often called on to play at weddings and funerals. She was a member of the Casa Grande Library Board for many years and served as Sunday school superintendent at the African American Methodist Episcopal Church. While records are unclear, she also may have taught for several years at a school in Stanfield, just west of Casa Grande.

One of her former students once said of her favorite teacher, "She was one of the most positive influences, other than my parents, in my life. She challenged all of us. She told us she expected great things from us."

Rebecca Dallis died in 1971. Among her possessions was a scrapbook of newspaper articles detailing the momentous 1954 *Brown v. Board of Education* decision of the U.S. Supreme Court, abolishing segregation.

In 1980, along with other notable Arizona women, Rebecca was chosen as one of the women for "Making a Difference: Arizona Women Building Communities, 1900–1980," sponsored in part by the Governor's Division for Women.

In 1992 the old Southside Colored Grammar School was relocated onto the grounds of the Casa Grande Valley Historical Society and Museum, and renamed the Rebecca Dallis Schoolhouse in honor of the woman who influenced the education of so many African American students.

"Preparing youth for citizenship is, after all, the whole sum and substance of education," she wrote, "and all of the efforts in whatever field we may work aim to contribute in some way toward that worthy end."

CORA LOUISE BOEHRINGER

[1878~1956]

Born in Morrison, Illinois, Cora Louise Boehringer was already a distinguished educator before moving to Yuma in 1912. Arizona, however, was completely different from her midwestern roots, and education was not yet a prominent issue.

Determined to raise educational standards for Arizona's children, she won the election for Yuma County school superintendent in 1913, serving for four years.

In 1917 she became editor and later owner of *The Arizona Teacher,* a journal she published for twenty years. The publication later served as the official handbook of the Arizona State Teachers Association.

Louise won a seat in the Arizona House of Representatives in 1920 and served two terms. As chair of the Education Committee, she initiated and developed statewide educational reforms such as establishing the state school board and securing permanent funding for Arizona's educational system. She believed her most important accomplishment was passage of a bill providing financial and educational support for illegitimate children.

She founded the Yuma chapter of the Business and Professional Women's Club, and in 1921 she was elected the first state president of the National Federation of Business and Professional Women's Clubs. She was president of the Arizona Council of Administrative Women in Education and served as chair of the Arizona State Federation of Women's Clubs. She also founded the Phoenix and Tucson branches of the National League of American Pen Women.

"There is no finer opportunity in life than that of teaching," she said when she ran for state superintendent of public instruction. After her third defeat, the "Mother of the Arizona educational system" retired to her alfalfa farm in Yuma. She died in Seattle, Washington, in 1956.

BUILDING BRIDGES

Maria Luisa Legarra Urquides

[1908–1994]

"**I** was born on a cold winter night by the light of an oil lamp. A *curandera* was in attendance, and my aunt…was accompanying my mother at my birth. She said I was born with a strange veil over my face. The curandera said this meant I would be able to tell the future."

Maria Luisa Legarra Urquides was born in Tucson on the evening of December 9, 1908. If she could tell the future, she would have foreseen her life unfolding very differently than that of her parents. Her father never attended school, and her mother did not go beyond the third grade. Yet their youngest child thrived in school, even though education of Mexican children in the Old Pueblo was far from perfect.

Schoolchildren were forbidden to speak any language but English. Those like Maria who knew only Spanish were often punished for conversing in their native tongue, even on the playground. Many youngsters spent two or three years in the first grade until they mastered the English language.

Initially, Maria did not feel the bias against her Mexican lineage "because we all needed each other so much. The Papago came in with the wood, pinole, *bellotas* [acorns], and tortillas to sell. And the Chinese parked their roving vegetable carts on the vacant land which my father owned."

By the time she entered first grade, Maria gained an even broader knowledge of her neighborhood when she went to work for the local prostitutes. "When they legalized prostitution in Gay Alley," she said, "it was right in back of our property. My dad quietly built a fence, but my curiosity was aroused and I loosened the boards and pushed in. Someone hollered 'Hi, Honey. Come on over.' So I got acquainted with the girls. I was running errands for them, getting good tips. That's the first time I ever had strawberries and cream with pink sugar."

"One afternoon I went to their door to see if they needed anything and one of them was hanging from a beam… I found her." When Maria's parents discovered her entrepreneurial enterprise, they moved.

Not until high school did she understand the disadvantages associated with her Mexican heritage. "In my junior and senior years, when I was into music, I began to notice that although I was friends with Anglo girls, I was never asked to go to their homes for parties." Plus, "The Mexican Americans decided I was being a *gringacita* [a disparaging word for a non-Hispanic person]."

With her father's words echoing in her ears, "Always do more than what is expected of you," Maria chose to further her education by going away to school. During this era, it was unheard of for Mexican girls to leave the safety and security of their homes until married. But with her parents' blessings she entered Arizona State Teachers College in Tempe (now Arizona State University), earning her way by cleaning toilets. Her singing voice finally landed her a job at a local restaurant.

In 1928 she graduated as valedictorian of her class and received her teaching certificate. That September she was hired to teach at Tucson's segregated Davis Elementary School. Her classroom consisted mainly of Mexican American and Yaqui Indian students. She taught subjects from music and art to ancient history, woodworking, and physical education.

For twenty years Maria educated the bilingual children at Davis School. She went to their homes to better understand their backgrounds and became an integral part of their lives. "She was the strongest encouragement I ever had to get ahead in life," said one of her former students. "Her close contact with our family gave us the encouragement to continue. She convinced my mother to keep us in school at all costs."

However, she was not allowed to teach the children in their native tongue, but had to hold class in English. "If I ever go to hell," she once said, "it'll be for scolding students for speaking Spanish."

After teaching her pupils to sing two Spanish-language songs for a spring festival, she was ordered to translate the songs into English. "That's how bad it was, but the only thing I could think was that this was the way it was done. It was the way I had learned."

Davis School received little money for improvements. When Maria decided to paint the dull gray walls of her classroom, she bought light green paint with her own funds and enlisted the help of her students to get the job done. To acquire shade trees for the barren playground, the children sold hot dogs and buns donated by Swift and Company. During the summer break, Maria asked the custodians to water the new trees, but when she returned in the fall they were all dead. The custodians had received orders not to waste money keeping the trees alive.

In 1948 she transferred to the predominately Anglo school, Sam Hughes Elementary. When she saw how beautifully the grounds were kept, the wonderful library available to the students, and the far superior education realized by these children, she questioned why the Davis and Hughes pupils could not know and learn from each other, enhancing the spectrum of their education. Her goal became to create a bilingual-bicultural teaching program.

MARIA LUISA LEGARRA URQUIDES

Over the years, Maria was involved with numerous neighborhood, city, and county activities and organizations. She was instrumental in establishing Tucson's Oury Park, located on land that once housed the town's horse-drawn vehicles. Along with neighbors Marian Lovett and Helena Patton, she talked the city fathers into turning the property into a recreational center. The three women formed Club Adelante, for Mexican American women interested in social and civic growth. Along with other improvements, they built a library, cleared a baseball field, and eventually acquired an auditorium and a swimming pool built with Works Progress Administration (WPA) funds, although Maria was disappointed when the pool was only open to black children the day before it was cleaned.

"Oh, how we scrubbed!" she remembered of the hard work cleaning off the property. "You can't imagine the trash and refuse which had accumulated, and I don't think the place had ever been cleaned! We begged, borrowed, and wheedled all the merchants in town into helping us by donating paint, material for curtains and that sort of thing, and the first thing we knew, the recreational center was a reality!"

While still teaching at Hughes, Maria and other teachers explored the idea of introducing bilingual education to their pupils. They surveyed other school districts in five southwestern states and wrote a report of their findings, "The Invisible Minority," which was published by the National Education Association.

Her reputation as one of the most effective advocates for bilingual education led President Harry S. Truman to appoint her to the White House Conference on Children and Youth in 1950.

Five years later, she left Hughes to teach at Tucson's new Pueblo High School, where her classes were mainly composed of Mexican teenagers unable to read or write their native language, and who knew little about their heritage. "It really bothered me at Pueblo to hear the students constantly prostituting their names by anglicizing them so that Anglo teachers could pronounce them more readily." She instructed her pupils to correct the teachers who mispronounced their Spanish names and began a concentrated effort to teach Spanish to Spanish-speaking students.

While teaching at Pueblo, she completed her master's degree in counseling at the University of Arizona and later took on the added task of the high school's dean of girls.

President Dwight D. Eisenhower reappointed her to the White House Conference on Children and Youth in 1960, and she was part of the Symposium on Bilingual Education held in Tucson in 1966. The symposium was so successful that members appeared before Congress to introduce the bilingual education concept.

During this time, President John F. Kennedy placed her on the Arizona State Advisory Committee to the Civil Rights Commission, and President Lyndon B. Johnson called on her to sit on the National Advisory Committee to the Commissioner of Education on Mexican-American Education.

In 1968 Congress passed the Bilingual Education Act, providing school districts with federal funds to establish educational programs for students with limited English-speaking abilities. The bill encouraged instruction in English while also promoting multicultural awareness. That first year, seventy-six bilingual education programs were initiated for students who spoke fourteen different languages.

Shortly after passage of the Bilingual Education Act, President Richard M. Nixon called on Maria, who by now had earned the title, "Mother of Bilingual Education," to once again sit on the White House Conference on Children and Youth.

Back in 1965, Maria had become the first woman to chair the Arizona State Board of Public Welfare (she was the only woman on the board). During the years, she participated in or led numerous organizations such as the YWCA, Tucson League of Mexican American Women, Tucson Education Association, Arizona Congress of Parents and Teachers, National Association for Advancement of Colored People, National Council of Christians and Jews, and the American Red Cross. She was a charter member of the Pima College Board of Governors and served on the Pima County Association for Juveniles, where she was instrumental in obtaining a separate area to hold detained children instead of having them incarcerated with adult inmates in the county jail.

In 1965 the League of Mexican American Women of Los Angeles named her Woman of the Year in Education. A scholarship was established in her name at the University of Arizona by the Mexican American Student Association. She received the Human Relations award from the National Education Association in 1968 and the Distinguished Service Award in 1970, followed by awards from both the University of Arizona and Pima Community College.

Although she retired from teaching in 1978, Maria continued to involve herself within the community. She was awarded an honorary doctor of law degree from the University of Arizona in 1983 for her work in education. That same year, President Ronald W. Reagan congratulated her for her service to Arizona and the nation.

And while she became involved in even more activities after her retirement, she also wished she "were just beginning to teach again."

"A Mexican-American child's ability to speak English has not automatically solved his education problems," she once said. "And helping does not mean changing the basic individuality but adding to it the knowledge and skills they will need to live their individual lives with others who are culturally different from them."

Maria's efforts to bring bilingual education into the classroom did not live up to her expectations. "Bilingual education is not what I hoped it would be—because we didn't teach the monolingual child, the Anglo child, to speak Spanish."

In 1984 she received the Medallion of Merit from the University of Arizona, only the fifth time the award had been given in the school's history. Arizona State University also gave her a Medallion of Excellence for her outstanding contributions to society. She received the YWCA Lifetime Achievement Award in 1989 and was honored as a pioneer by the National Association for Bilingual Education in 1990. Maria was inducted into the Hispanic Hall of Fame and the Arizona Women's Hall of Fame.

She died on June 16, 1994, but her contributions to education continue to resonate throughout schools in Arizona as well as across the country. "Maria's ceaseless devotion to improving the lot of all children has made a lasting impact on the lives of thousands of young people," Arizona Monsignor Thomas P. Cahalane once remarked. "Her belief in the ultimate goodness of people helped her build a bridge between people of all races."

WOMEN OF THE ARTS

outh of Flagstaff, on the twisting trail known as Route 89A, designated a U.S. Scenic Route complete with switchbacks and breathtaking views, the cutoff for Jerome takes one to an old mining town perched precariously on a hillside overlooking ore tailings from lucrative days past. Katie Lee's house is easy to spot, clinging to the sloping precipice, with its bright blue exterior and a sign above the door commanding all to "Sing." She has already celebrated beyond her ninetieth birthday and still has fire in her words and tears in her eyes when she talks about the 1950s flooding of Glen Canyon. Katie is an artist of words and music. She expresses her thoughts and ideals through her books and songs.

Sharlot Hall and Martha Summerhayes also used their written voices to proclaim the wonders, and the hardships, of living in early Arizona Territory. Through her poetry Sharlot left a myriad of images describing Arizona's past. As the territory's first historian, she was determined Arizona would stand unfettered as a state, and she used the power of her pen to help accomplish that goal.

Martha Summerhayes spent just a few years in Arizona, but her written adventures while accompanying her army officer husband from one military camp to another offer insight into the lives of women who followed the military into dangerous, often uncharted western lands. A collection of Martha's old recipes, which she gathered as she traipsed across the country, is housed at the Arizona History Museum in Tucson.

Native American women have been creating artwork for thousands of years. Hopi potter Nampeyo left a magnificent collection of earthenware vessels to touch and admire. She used native materials that made her pottery unique, and even blindness could not deter her from designing artifacts with an intricacy seldom duplicated today. Her legacy continues through the talents of her extensive family.

The paintbrushes of Kate Cory illustrate true treasures of Arizona's past. Kate's vibrant portraits of the Hopi people show her love of these proud individuals with whom she lived for many years. Her use of oils and soft watercolors bring out the richness of the Hopi lifestyle.

On a grand scale, Mary Colter built impressive edifices to honor the indigenous people of the West. Her architectural style fits comfortably into the natural setting of the Grand Canyon, and her use of local minerals and materials, along with ancient designs, reflect the history of the region without destroying its beauty and grandeur. The buildings she created are majestic monuments to ancient cultures.

The ruggedness of the West is often glorified in stories and art depicting the rough, tough cowboy riding off into the sunset. It is the beauty of the sunset, however, that is remembered through the ages. Artistry in its many forms makes us think, sing, dance, and enjoy the wonders of the world. Those who leave these creative legacies are the handmaidens of our minds and souls.

FRONTIER LITERATURE

Martha Dunham Summerhayes

[1846–1911]

Martha Dunham Summerhayes spent four years in Arizona, returning for a brief stay ten years later. During these times, she formed very definite opinions about this untamed territory. She wrote about her experiences in her book, *Vanished Arizona: Recollections of the Army Life of a New England Woman*, first published in 1908.

Born into a wealthy family on Nantucket Island, Massachusetts, on October 21, 1846, Martha knew little about military life until she married John "Jack" Wyer Summerhayes, a career army man, on March 16, 1874, and immediately set out for Fort Russell in Wyoming Territory. By August she was on the steamship *Newbern* out of San Francisco, headed for Fort Yuma, Arizona Territory. From there, she began her adventures across barren and desolate terrain from one military post to another.

The nearly month-long trip to Yuma was so disagreeable, Martha actually welcomed the sight of the desert fort as it came into view. "I can never forget the taste of the oatmeal with fresh milk, the eggs and butter, and delicious tomatoes," she remembered of her first breakfast in town.

Boarding a boat for a trip up the Colorado River, she related, "I felt, somehow, as though we were saying good-bye to the world and civilization, and as our boat clattered and tugged away up river with its great wheel astern, I could not help looking back longingly to old Fort Yuma."

As they approached the shores of Ehrenberg, "visions of castles on the Rhine, and stories of the Middle Ages floated through my mind, as I sprang up, in pleasurable anticipation of seeing an interesting and beautiful place. Alas! for my ignorance. I saw but a row of low thatched hovels, perched on the edge of the ragged looking river-bank... Of all the dreary, miserable-looking settlements that one could possibly imagine, that was the worst."

Dallying no more than a few days in Ehrenberg, the ship sailed upriver to Camp Mojave. From there, Martha settled into a Dougherty wagon for the bone-jolting ride to Fort Whipple.

At the first campsite along the trail, Jack introduced her to a soldier named Bowen, who was assigned to help with chores and cooking. Martha was stymied about what to prepare for dinner in this godforsaken place and meekly asked where she could find eggs. Bowen quickly replied, "Oh, you don't need eggs; you're on the frontier now; you must learn to do without eggs."

Martha often wrote about the food she encountered and her inability to cook. "Like all New England girls of that period, I knew how to make quince jelly and floating islands, but of the actual, practical side of cooking, and the management of a range, I knew nothing." When she complained about the lack of kitchen utensils she had to work with, her husband said she was "pampered and spoiled... [Y]ou will have to learn to do as other army women do—cook in cans and such things, be inventive, and learn to do with nothing."

After sighting her first rattlesnake, Martha watched fearfully as Bowen surrounded her mattress with a braided horsehair lariat. He told her snakes would not cross over the flimsy barrier but she slept very little that first night.

Arriving in Fort Whipple, the party lingered briefly before heading out for Camp Verde and on to Camp Apache. Days blurred into weeks. Martha found the land "positively hostile in its attitude towards every living thing except snakes, centipedes and spiders." As they crossed the Mogollon Rim, fresh catches of deer and turkey made the journey a little more tolerable, but the fear of Indian attacks kept Martha on edge.

Once settled at Camp Apache, she was daunted by the task of finding a place for everything in her cramped quarters. She went to see a Mrs. Bailey to ask her advice how to cope in this wild land. "To my surprise, I found her out playing tennis, her little boy asleep in the baby-carriage." Such civility in the outback of Arizona astounded Martha, and she "decided then and there that young army wives should stay at home with their mothers and fathers, and not go into such wild and uncouth places." Yet she adored Jack Summerhayes and "where he was, was home to me."

In January 1875 Martha gave birth to Harry R. Summerhayes at Camp Apache. Typical of the times, she mentioned nothing in her book about the impending pregnancy except to say she "could not go out very much at that time."

About a week after Harry's birth, a group of Native American women called on Martha and presented her with a cradleboard for the newborn. "This was made of the lightest wood," she said, "and covered with the finest skin of fawn, tanned with birch bark by their own hands, and embroidered in blue beads; it was their best work."

That April, Jack received orders to report to Camp McDowell. Martha bundled up baby Harry, buckled a small holstered derringer around her waist, and boarded the wagon for the long journey. She had not yet regained her strength and dreaded leaving the fort's doctor, even though he was "much better versed in the sawing off of soldiers' legs than in the treatment of young mothers and babies."

Danger lurked behind every boulder. At one point, the travelers had to maneuver through Sanford's Pass, notorious for concealing raiding Apaches. As they made their way into the pass, Jack warned Martha that if he were shot, she should use her derringer on both herself and the baby rather than be kidnapped by the marauders. "Don't let them get either of you alive," he warned. Fortunately, the pass lay empty. On the other side, Jack whipped out his flask and all enjoyed a good cup of whiskey.

As the party careened down the mountains into Beaver Springs, Martha clung to little Harry. "I had been brought up in a flat country down near the sea, and I did not know the dangers of mountain travelling, nor the difficulties attending the piloting of a six-mule team down a road... I seemed also to be realizing that the Southwest was a great country and that there was much to learn about. Life out there was beginning to interest me."

Shortly after arriving at Camp Whipple, Jack informed Martha they would not be going on to Camp McDowell, but would instead head back to Ehrenberg, a totally unbearable place to live as far as she was concerned. As they drove once again across the desert, one of the men killed a rattlesnake and offered the rattles to little Harry as a toy. The gritty desert crept into Martha's psyche. "It seemed so white, so bare, so endless, and so still; irreclaimable, eternal, like Death itself."

On May 16, 1875, the army ambulance rattled into Ehrenberg, still desolate, still afire with the blazing sun. Martha decided the best place for her and

MARTHA DUNHAM SUMMERHAYES

little Harry that summer was San Francisco. She boarded the boat for the trip downriver, but by the time she reached the mouth of the Colorado, she was ready to return to whatever lay before her upriver. "Ehrenberg had become truly my old man of the sea; I could not get rid of it. There I must go, and there I must stay, until circumstances and the Fates were more propitious for my departure."

Summer in Ehrenberg turned out to be rather pleasant. Martha enlarged her living quarters and learned how to make tortillas, although she claimed she never mastered the technique. She devoured frijoles cooked by Mexican women and learned terms such as "*carni seca* [*sic*]" and "*chile verde.*" As she "sweltered during the day in high-necked and long-sleeved white dresses," she envied her Mexican neighbors' loose-fitting clothing styles. "Oh! If I could only dress as the Mexicans do! Their necks and arms do look so cool and clean." At dawn she often waded into the Colorado River to bathe rather than sit in a tub full of the same muddy water.

By winter, she was comfortable in her surroundings and took pleasure in the magnificent Arizona sunsets. "I have never seen anything like that wonderful color, which spread itself over sky, river and desert. For an hour, one could have believed oneself in a magician's realm."

Martha and Harry visited Nantucket in the spring of 1876, but by winter, she was ready to return to Arizona. "I had discovered that I was really a soldier's wife and I must go back to it all. To the army with its glitter and its misery, to the post with its discomforts, to the soldiers, to the drills, to the bugle-calls, to the monotony, to the heat of Southern Arizona, to the uniform and the stalwart Captains and gay Lieutenants who wore it, I felt the call and I must go."

Jack was now stationed at Fort McDowell. Martha found the journey back to Arizona almost a delight and wondered "if I had really grown to love the desert." The summer heat soon convinced her otherwise. Stifling temperatures made sleeping indoors impossible. She bathed in the waters of the Verde River that were "almost as thick as that of the Great Colorado."

In June 1878 Jack was sent to Fort Lowell near Tucson, but as soon they arrived, he was immediately ordered back to Fort McDowell, then to California. As she crossed from Arizona Territory into the California desert, Martha looked back and "felt sorry that the old days had come to an end."

In 1879 Katherine Summerhayes was born in Nantucket, and Martha remembered the difficult times at Fort Apache four years earlier when she had given birth to Harry.

Ordered back to Arizona in 1886, Martha and her family enjoyed the luxury of traveling by train into Tucson. "Everything seemed changed," she remarked to Jack, "This isn't the same Arizona we knew in '74. I don't believe I like it as well either; all this luxury doesn't seem to belong to this place."

Assigned to Fort Lowell, their duty lasted from July to November, which was the last time Martha set foot in Arizona. Yet she never forgot the adventures, fears, and discoveries as she traveled the width and breadth of this wild new frontier.

Jack Summerhayes died in March 1911; Martha followed him on May 12 that same year. Both were buried in Arlington National Cemetery, home to the nation's war heroes.

Martha wrote *Vanished Arizona* at the urging of family and friends. It was reprinted in 1911, shortly before her death.

"I did not see much to admire in the desolate waste lands," she recalled as she penned her memoirs. "I did not dream of the power of the desert, nor that I should ever long to see it again. But as I write, the longing possesses me, and the pictures then indelibly printed upon my mind, long forgotten amidst the scenes and events of half a lifetime, unfold themselves like a panorama before my vision and call me to come back, to look upon them once more."

PRESERVING THE PAST

Sharlot Mabridth Hall

[1870–1943]

Morning does not come in the desert as it comes in other lands. There is an hour of pale, dust-sifted light, always increasing, before the sun comes. An hour when the earth seems wrapped in mystery; and the air has a faint, other-worldly fragrance, haunting and intangible, like a breath of incense blown through some still, far-doomed temple."

Sharlot Mabridth Hall breathed in the desert air as she and her family traveled by wagon from Kansas to Arizona in late 1881. She later wrote of her experience in the short story, "The Fruit of the Yucca Tree," published by *Out West* magazine in 1905. It was one of dozens of stories, articles, and poems she created for editor Charles Fletcher Lummis starting in the late 1800s, a very productive time in her literary career, one she had journeyed a great distance to achieve.

Born in Lincoln County, Kansas, on October 17, 1870, Sharlot was eleven years old when her family made the thousand-mile journey to Arizona Territory. Charged with keeping a herd of twenty thoroughbred horses under control, her eyes constantly darted across the ever-changing landscape as the wagon train made its way along the Santa Fe Trail. She watched the countryside morph from wheat-swept plains into mauve-tinged mountains, then merge into the vast southwestern desert. Pen in hand, the young poet composed as she rode, the unfolding scenery a scroll for her words and verse.

The only flaw in this wondrous adventure was a fall Sharlot took from her horse, in which she suffered a spinal injury that would plague her the rest of her life.

James Hall, Sharlot's father, eventually settled his family on 160 acres in Lonesome Valley near present-day Dewey, eking out a living raising cattle and growing fruit trees on his Orchard Ranch.

Sharlot and her brother Ted attended school in Agua Fria, but most of their time was spent working on the ranch. Adeline Hall encouraged her children in their educational pursuits, but her husband had no use for book learning. After one semester of high school in nearby Prescott, Sharlot returned to the ranch, her school days at an end, but not her literary pursuits.

At age twenty-one, she first saw her words in print when the children's magazine *Wide Awake* published her short story, "The Genesis of the Earth and Moon: A Moqui Folk Tale."

Showing a keen interest in photography, she usually carried a camera, along with paper and pen, to record her observations. By 1892, however, she was in excruciating pain from the back injury she had sustained when she fell from her horse twelve years earlier. Immobile for months, she wrote diligently.

Her solitude was rewarded the following year when the Denver publication *The Great Divide* ran her poem "A Border Tale," followed by a short story, "Tailing, a Tramp." That same year, *The Archaeologist* published her description of a trip to the Verde Valley.

In good health once again, Sharlot spent the summer of 1893 exploring Arizona while gathering information for additional articles. From this trip, she later completed two articles about the Grand Canyon and a short story, "A Christmas at the Grand Cañon."

In 1895 she met Freethinker Samuel Porter Putnam, and a romance blossomed even though Putnam was thirty years her senior. After he left town, Sharlot took up the cause of Freethinking, the belief that opinions should be formed based on science, logic, and reason, and not influenced by authority, tradition, or any other principle.

The relationship was short-lived. A year later Putnam and a woman died in a hotel room, both victims of a leaky gas pipe. For the next several years, Sharlot wrote some of her most moving poetry about death and lost loves, including "Alone," and "The Silent Leader."

Throughout this time, she contributed numerous poems, stories, and articles to Charles Lummis's California publication *Land of Sunshine,* gaining national exposure for her work. By 1901 she was listed as one of the magazine's contributing editors. Within a few years her name appeared on the masthead as associate editor.

When Lummis renamed his publication *Out West,* he recruited Sharlot to write for the first issue. One of her most rewarding accomplishments was the poem she composed, "Out West." Lummis had the poem mounted on heavy cardboard and distributed across the country, both to advertise his new magazine and to provide a wider audience for Sharlot's work.

Her reputation grew as other periodicals such as *Atlantic Monthly, Ladies' Home Journal, Sunset,* and *The Delineator* published the words of the up-and-coming Arizona poet and journalist. Working steadily over the next few years, she composed some of her best work, including "The Mercy of Nah-né," which has been lauded as one of her most compelling poems. The ballad tells the story of a gambler who valiantly, and vainly, fought off Apache warriors to save his family.

While working with Charles Lummis, Sharlot gathered stories from Arizona pioneers, collected relics of early Arizona days, spoke to gatherings, and encouraged old-timers to write down their stories and "save everything."

In December 1905 President Theodore Roosevelt recommended Arizona and New Mexico be admitted to the Union as one state under the Hamilton Bill. Sharlot adamantly opposed this proposition. Taking pen in hand, she composed a resounding tribute to the territory that had been her home for over thirty years. Her ballad "Arizona" landed on the desk of every member of the U.S. Congress, proclaiming Arizona's right to stand alone as a sovereign state.

The bill passed through the House of Representatives, but before the Senate approved it, the language for joint statehood was removed. Several newspapers gave Sharlot credit for assisting in the defeat of the bill. Pennsylvania's *Morning Courier* suggested, "Sharlot M. Hall perhaps put out the strongest papers that were issued to show why Arizona should, when admitted to statehood, be admitted as a great commonwealth singly."

She must have enjoyed her brush with politics, for in 1907 she ran for and won a clerk position in the 25th Arizona Territorial Legislature. Governor Joseph H. Kibbey used her expertise to help write legislation to improve Arizona's chances for statehood.

By 1908 she had left her editorial position with *Out West* to seek reelection, but failed to regain her position.

When Governor Richard E. Sloan appointed her territorial historian in 1909, the first woman to hold a public office in Arizona, Sharlot was delighted to

SHARLOT MABRIDTH HALL

continue her work with Arizona's pioneers. She scoured public records and old newspapers for information on early Arizona and roamed the state amassing remnants of Arizona's past while listening to stories about pioneering on the western frontier.

In 1910 she put together a collection of her poetry and saw her first book, *Cactus and Pine: Songs of the Southwest,* come to fruition. She included the ballad "Out West" that she had written for the first issue of Charles Lummis's publication, her celebrated poem "The Mercy of Nah-né" (retitled "The Mercy of Na-Chis"), and "Arizona," her rousing tribute to separate statehood.

As part of her historian duties, Sharlot set out in 1911 to explore the Arizona Strip, a piece of land extending from the southern end of the Grand Canyon to the Utah border. Her purpose was "to gather all the historical data possible, as well as to inform myself about the country and conditions..." Utah wanted to acquire this portion of Arizona Territory, arguing it was more than three hundred miles to Flagstaff while only eight miles to Kanab.

The journal she maintained throughout the expedition was published in *Arizona, The New State Magazine* from December 1911 through April 1913, and compiled into a book after her death, *A Diary of a Journey through Northern Arizona in 1911: Sharlot Hall on the Arizona Strip.*

She traveled by buckboard through some of the most remote regions of the territory with only a guide for company. Recording her thoughts as well as the sights and people she saw along the way, she was captivated with the image of an old Paiute woman. "She looked like Age on a journey... [H]er dull eyes looked like bits of agate in the gnarled old face that had little human about it."

Paiute children struck her as ragged and undernourished, "Their thin little bodies looked like hard times on the range."

She traipsed across this desolate land for seventy-five days. Arriving in Kingman, she declared that she "did indeed say some prayers of gladness—for a thousand miles in a camp wagon is no joke, even when every day is filled with interest and the quest of fresh historical game."

Sharlot and the rest of Arizona celebrated admission to the Union on February 14, 1912, yet statehood eliminated her position as territorial historian. That same year, Adeline Hall died, and Sharlot was left alone with her petulant father. For the next ten years she wrote little, as her days were consumed with running Orchard Ranch.

Looking up from her chores one day, she found a handful of prominent Prescott businessmen standing at her doorstep. They had formed the Smoki People, an organization dedicated to preserving Native American ceremonies and rites, and asked Sharlot to write a fictional account of their origins. The creative spark that had been dimmed for the past decade was rekindled as Sharlot penned *The Story of the Smoki People* in 1922, the "results so artistic and pleasing that it awoke a very old dream of mine to write again."

Friends encouraged her to republish *Cactus and Pine*, which was then out of print, and to include additional poems she had composed since its issuance. She agreed, but argued "so many are only what one busy woman on a remote little ranch thought and saw."

Since her first publisher had gone out of business, she asked a friend to locate the original plates. "He wrote me that all of the metal, including my plates, had been sold to a munitions factory [during World War I], and that so far as he could learn my poems had been shot at the Hun, and, we might hope, had done their part in winning the war in a decidedly original way for poetry."

She had plans to produce additional volumes, including *Poems of a Ranchwoman* and *A Woman of the Old Frontier*. Only *Poems* was published after her death.

When President Calvin Coolidge was elected in 1924, Sharlot, an elector for the Republican Party, was chosen to carry Arizona's votes to the Electoral College in Washington D.C. She wore a dress made of Arizona copper for the occasion, complete with a small copper purse and a hat adorned with cactus. "I felt like Cinderella…" she gushed, recounting how she waited in the reception line to greet the president.

James Hall died in 1925, freeing Sharlot to live life on her own terms. Having amassed a vast array of Arizona memorabilia, she sought to house her collection in the first governor's mansion, built in 1864 for Territorial Governor John Goodwin. The log cabin had been given to the City of Prescott in 1917, but the old structure was in a state of stagnant disrepair.

City fathers were more than happy to turn over the project of restoring the mansion to Sharlot and gave her a lifetime lease on the property. Selling Orchard Ranch, she moved into the dilapidated building and for the next fourteen years worked tirelessly to refurbish the house to its original grandeur.

She produced booklets about Arizona pioneers to raise money for the museum. In 1935 she composed "A House of a Thousand Hands," describing the buildings and people who had made her dream of a house of history materialize.

Her heart gave out on April 9, 1943, before she had finished all she hoped to accomplish. Yet her legacy continues.

"It is my one wish," Sharlot wrote in her will, "that the work I have begun be carried on after my death, to the end that the old gubernatorial mansion may be preserved in its present condition and may become a shrine dedicated to the preservation of the pioneer life and history of Arizona."

Sharlot got her wish for the mansion, along with the grounds on which it stands, was renamed Sharlot Hall Museum, honoring the woman whom Arizona Governor Sidney P. Osborn proclaimed at her funeral was "one of the grandest characters that ever lived in our state."

ARCHITECTURE AND ARCHAEOLOGY

Mary Elizabeth Jane Colter

[1869–1958]

Twenty-two women architects were listed on the 1890 U.S. Census. One of them was Mary Elizabeth Jane Colter, who had just graduated from the California School of Design. Having already lost her father, the twenty-one-year-old vowed to help support her mother and sister if allowed to attend the prestigious art school. Now she had to fulfill that promise.

Born in Pittsburgh, Pennsylvania, on April 4, 1869, Mary was eleven years old when the family returned to their roots in St. Paul, Minnesota. Three years later, the prodigious student graduated from high school. After attaining her degree from the California School of Design, she returned to St. Paul and taught high school freehand and mechanical drawing for the next fifteen years.

She was thirty-three years old in 1902, when she acquired her first job as an interior designer for the Fred Harvey Company, developer of hotels, dining establishments, and gift shops lining the newly built Atchison, Topeka, and Santa Fe Railway lines. Harvey's fleet of waitresses, known as Harvey Girls, became famous for their hospitality, cleanliness, and attention to detail. Fred died in 1901, but the company continued to operate into the 1960s.

In 1904 the Harvey Company hired Mary to design a building across from the El Tovar Hotel at the Grand Canyon to house Native American arts and crafts.

Mary determined to build an authentic-looking, multistoried Hopi dwelling using local limestone and sandstone. The concrete interior flooring of Hopi House looked like dried mud, while chimneys rose from stacks of broken ollas (pots) mortared together. Two layers of small branches held up with vigas (log beams) created the ceiling. Initially visitors took ladders from the central room to the two floors above.

Mary draped handwoven Navajo blankets and rugs across rustic wooden tables and benches. Woven Pomo baskets hung from the ceiling, while Hopi pottery competed for space with woodcarvings and religious artifacts. A welcoming fireplace allowed visitors to sit and watch potters, basket weavers, and jewelers fashion their fine art.

When Hopi House opened on January 1, 1905, Native American families were invited to stay there while demonstrating their arts and crafts. The first artist to visit was Nampeyo, considered one of the finest Hopi potters of her time.

With Hopi House complete, Mary returned to her teaching position until 1908, when she acquired a job designing sections of the Frederick and Nelson Department Store in Seattle, Washington. She relocated her mother, Rebecca, and sister Harriet to Seattle, but the dwindling family returned to St. Paul in 1909 after Rebecca's death.

In 1910 the Harvey Company hired Mary as a permanent architect and interior designer. Both the Harvey Company and the Santa Fe Railway employed her, since the railroad held title to the land and buildings she worked on, while the Harvey Company owned the contents of the structures. She moved to Harvey headquarters in Kansas City, Missouri, and almost immediately set off for Lamy, New Mexico, just south of Santa Fe, to design the interior of El Ortiz Hotel. By 1914 she was back at the Grand Canyon, working on two different projects.

In the early days, the Harvey Company carted sightseers along the south rim of the canyon in horse-drawn wagons. At the end of the eight-mile run, tourists needed a place to stop and rest while enjoying the majestic views. Mary built Hermit's Rest to resemble an old prospector's shack almost buried in the rock, blending with the surroundings and looking like a pile of boulders and timber ready to collapse, disheveled yet homey. On the roof, plants sprouted and were encouraged to grow.

Inside, she created a massive arched fireplace and blackened the fireplace ceiling to make it look soot-ravaged and aged. A large bearskin rug lay on the hearth. She designed heavy tables and chairs, some hollowed from old tree trunks. The dark yet inviting interior roused comments, and when asked why she did not brighten it up, Mary gleefully replied, "You can't imagine what it cost to make it look this old."

Lookout Studio was also built as if naturally jutting out along a teetering ledge of the canyon. Designed for sightseers to view and photograph the canyon from the most advantageous positions, Lookout Studio consists of large stones randomly placed into the walls, complementing the irregular roofline. She meticulously placed what seemed like a pile of rubble at the base of the chimney and encouraged native plants to grow amid the rocky landscape.

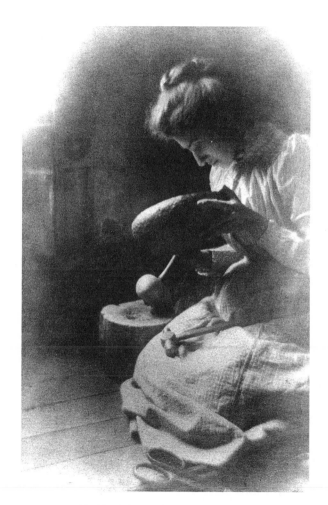

MARY ELIZABETH JANE COLTER

Exposed interior walls and a timber-framed ceiling surround the arched stone fireplace hidden in an alcove. A small staircase sends visitors upward for more distant views and to utilize strategically placed high-powered telescopes and binoculars. A Harvey brochure described Lookout Studio as "a tiny rustic club…with its bright-hued Navaho rugs, electric lights, cozy fireplace and many easy chairs."

With the completion of these buildings, Mary established herself as one of the leading architects in America's national parks. She traveled to ancient ruins by horse and wagon, auto, and even by plane, an uncommon conveyance at the time, to study prehistoric architecture that allowed her to merge Native American culture and artistry with early frontier history.

Her next project took her to Gallup, New Mexico, to design El Navajo Hotel and railway station. Departing from the cozy, lived-in look of her Grand Canyon structures, Mary produced a stark yet decidedly Native American appearance at the Gallup hotel. "I have always longed to carry out the true Indian idea," she said, "to plan a hotel strictly Indian with none of the conventionalized modern motifs." The hotel initially opened in 1918, with a second phase added in 1923.

Called back to the Grand Canyon, Mary headed to the canyon floor to design Phantom Ranch, a stopping-off place for hardy visitors who trekked up and down the steep trails on their own two feet or on sure-footed mules. Since everything but native stone had to be hauled in by pack mule, she designed a simple lodge, kitchen, and dining room amid a cluster of green-roofed cabins. Yet each sparsely furnished cabin boasted a fireplace and brightly colored Indian floor rugs.

Mary and her sister rode down the Kaibab trail when Phantom Ranch opened in 1922. Harriet had never enjoyed the health and stamina of her younger sister, and when she died the following year, Mary took her back to St. Paul to be buried next to their parents.

She decorated various Harvey facilities at railroad stations in Kansas City, Chicago, St. Louis, and Los Angeles. She designed the interior of La Fonda Hotel in Santa Fe in 1926, before returning to Arizona to design the railway station and La Posada ("the inn") in Winslow, one of her most detailed and demanding compositions.

The muted-pink stucco La Posada hotel rose only two stories but rambled across the desert, accommodating seventy guest rooms and five suites. She placed tiled linoleum on the floors to cushion footsteps outside oak-planked doors. Each room sported a Mexican or Indian rug, and those with fireplaces sprouted brightly painted flowers and vines above the mantles.

Much of the furniture was built on site under Mary's supervision. Simple tables, chairs, and rustic benches were built to resemble antiques, like the two-hundred-year-old chest she uncovered in a Winslow ranch house, and the aging

Mexican church pew she placed in the lounge next to the fireplace. Many of the wall motifs came from old church altars and *retablos* (devotional artwork, usually painted on wood).

U-shaped lunchroom counters displayed Spanish tiles splayed with fanciful geometric patterns and flowers, while the arched-windowed dining room sat beneath a rough log-beamed ceiling. Dining tables covered in gold-colored linen held fine china housed in oversized wooden hutches. Finding the Harvey Girls' dark dresses and pristine white aprons too drab for the colorful desert oasis she had created, Mary provided the female staff with multicolored quilted aprons, adding to the festive atmosphere of La Posada.

She built a wall around the hotel like those once used to deter invaders—much in the style of old Spanish haciendas—even adding loopholes for imaginary rifles. She designed gardens with fountains and planted elm, cottonwood, poplar, juniper, and fruit trees. She gathered and scattered specimens from the Petrified Forest before it was forbidden to remove these artistic objects from the park.

La Posada opened on May 15, 1930, during the throes of the Great Depression and stock market crash. Santa Fe officials sent a telegram to the Harvey people congratulating them on the stunning hotel they had created, adding the comment, "Hope income exceeds estimates as much as the building costs did."

With La Posada completed, Mary turned her attention back to the Grand Canyon to create an observation tower on the South Rim. "First and most important," she said, "was to design a building that would become a part of its surroundings—one that would create no discordant note against the time eroded walls of this promontory."

She became fascinated with the remnants of round stone towers found among ancient Indian ruins, even flying over some of these precipices to obtain one view, then hiking far inland to see the towering protuberances firsthand.

Desert View Watchtower is an engineering wonder. The steel-framed spire rises seventy feet above the canyon walls, anchored on a concrete base that Mary camouflaged with large boulders. The building houses three levels reached by a winding staircase. On the first floor she designed a bench cut from a tree trunk and crafted an owl stool from a tree root. Chairs were covered in rawhide. She filled the second floor with paintings of animals, people, and objects of her own design. She left the top-floor Eagle's Nest almost bare, allowing the wonders of the canyon to be viewed without distraction.

Mary was a tough taskmaster on this project, demanding work be torn down and redone if it did not meet her expectations. Hopi painter Fred Kabotie did much of the artwork and remembered that he and Mary did not always agree, "but I think we appreciated each other."

As soon as Desert View Watchtower opened, Mary began planning Bright Angel Lodge, along the rim of the canyon, completed in 1935. One of the most striking elements of the hotel is a massive fireplace in which she incorporated the full strata of stone that makes up the canyon. Colorado River rocks form the base and hearth. Vishnu Schist, Muav Limestone, Redwall Limestone, Hermit Shale, and Coconino Sandstone layers reach to the topmost Kaibab Limestone taken from the canyon's rim.

Always adding her own special touches, she painted the interior of the lodge a specific shade of blue that became known as "Mary Jane Blue," and converted old oil lamps into electric lights.

Shortly after the hotel was completed, Mary designed two dormitories for Bright Angel employees, the last of her architectural projects, although she often returned to sites she had previously designed for remodeling tasks.

In 1937 the Santa Fe Railway initiated its luxury Super Chief line between Chicago and Los Angeles, and asked Mary to create a china pattern for the Native American-inspired dining cars. She fashioned tableware from designs created in the thirteenth century by New Mexico Mimbreño Indians. The reddish geometric borders surrounded animal figures on ivory-colored dishes that she insisted had to look handmade. She discarded those that were too cleanly drawn.

In 1948, shortly after redecorating the Painted Desert Inn just outside of Holbrook, Mary retired from the Fred Harvey Company. The company, however, still needed her expertise. In 1949 she remodeled the cocktail lounge at La Fonda.

Suffering a fall and broken hip in 1955, she spent her last years confined to a wheelchair. Mary died January 8, 1958, at age eighty-nine. She was buried next to her family in St. Paul.

Mary Jane Colter instilled a new form of architecture and design into the profusion of buildings she created, particularly at Grand Canyon National Park, yet her name appears on very few of the architectural plans and drawings. The magnificence of her unique details and drawings and her ability to adapt architecture to nature as well as ancient civilizations is a legacy that will remain through the ages.

CLAY MAGIC

Nampeyo

[CIRCA 1860–1942]

Nampeyo spun the clay between her hands, forming a long coil. Placing the coil on a flattened clay bottom, she wound it up and around, pressing gently as she worked, so the clay rope would adhere. A second coil was added, then a third, until the Hopi woman had formed the shape and size she desired. Taking a gourd she smoothed the surface of the newly formed pot inside and out, left the pot to dry in the sun, then rubbed it with fine sandstone. She polished the vessel with a flat wet stone before preparing the paints to decorate the container.

She mixed red, white, and dark brown minerals with water. Beeweed or mustard plants boiled to a thick syrup provided black tones. Nampeyo chewed the ends of fibrous yucca plants to make fine brushes for delicate strokes, while swabs of sheep's wool produced wide swipes of color across the bowl.

Dried sheep dung formed the firing pit. She placed her pots on rocks around the hot fire and shielded them from the flames with shards of broken pottery. Sometimes she used sheep bones to intensify the heat of the kiln. She completed the oven by building a dome of dung over the pots, and left them to burn for several hours.

Brushing ashes from the fired pots, she carefully removed them from the dung-kiln before wiping them clean. They were now ready for use or sale.

Nampeyo, from the village of Hano on First Mesa of the Hopi community, was born around 1860, the fourth child and first daughter of Ko'icheve of the Hopi Snake Clan and Qotca Ka-o (White Corn) of the Tewa Corn Clan (spellings vary on both her parents' names). At puberty, she was given the Tewa name "Nung-beh-yong," usually pronounced "Nahm-PAY-oh" by outsiders.

As a child, she learned pottery making from her paternal grandmother; the artistic skills of the craft had almost gone out of existence over the centuries. Nampeyo is credited with reviving ancient Sikyátki pottery designs and redefining them with her own imaginative techniques.

In 1875 a small group of men led by photographer William Henry Jackson arrived at First Mesa. Nampeyo's brother, Tom Polacca, a respected leader and liaison between the Hopis and outside visitors, welcomed them, as he was one of

NAMPEYO

the few Hopis who spoke English. With Jackson traveled a correspondent for the *New York Times*, E. A. Barber. "Scarcely had we become seated," Barber reported, "when a beautiful girl approached and placed before us a large mat heaped with pee-kee, or bread."

> She was of short stature and plump, but not unbecoming so. Her eyes were almond shape, coal black, and possessed a voluptuous expression, which made them extremely fascinating. Her hair was arranged in…two large puffs, which, although odd to us, nevertheless seemed to enhance her beauty… [E]very movement of her head or exquisitely molded hands and arms or bare little feet was one of faultless grace… We had entered abruptly and awkwardly enough, with our hats unremoved…but on the approach of the modest and beautiful Nun-pa-yu… [E]very head was uncovered in a movement…

Barber's heart was not the only one that fluttered for teenage Nampeyo. The following year she married a Tewa man named Kwivioya, but the union was short lived. Legend claims Kwivioya was so in awe of her beauty that he abandoned her rather than lose her to another man and live in disgrace. In 1878 she married Lesou (or Lesso) of the Cedarwood clan from Walpi. From 1884 to 1900, she bore six children. While raising her family, she also produced some of her most artistic and innovative work.

Nampeyo's pottery differed greatly from that of most Hopi potters of the time. Seeking out specific clays and the raw materials needed for color, she preferred to shape low, wide pots with abstract, geometric designs flowing freely across the container, both inside and out. She did not fill her bowls with detail, but used space as an art form as well as intricate brush strokes and bold splashes of color. Her work was later compared with that of twentieth-century cubist artist Pablo Picasso.

When anthropologist Ruth Bunzel interviewed her in the mid-1920s, Nampeyo described the placement of her designs. "The best arrangement for the water jar is four designs around the top, two and two, like this," said the potter as she drew a diagram on the ground. "The designs opposite each other should be alike."

In the early 1900s, the Fred Harvey Company hired Mary Colter to design Hopi House, a sixty- by ninety-foot edifice built by Hopi workmen to resemble a typical Hopi dwelling—three stories high with pole ladders ascending to each terrace.

Hopi artisans were invited to Hopi House to demonstrate their crafts of weaving, basketry, jewelry, and pottery making, and to sell their products to the public. Nampeyo and her family were the first to arrive in January 1905. The family stayed for three months while Nampeyo and her firstborn daughter Annie crafted pottery. They were so successful that they ran out of clay. Since Nampeyo would only use clays from certain areas, Harvey employees had to send for more from the reservation.

Since she could not write, Nampeyo never signed her pottery. Harvey employees placed a small black and gold sticker on the bottom of her pots identifying the artist. Today, many pots are erroneously sold under Nampeyo's name, but those that contain this tiny identification seal indicate a possibility of authenticity and are widely coveted as true works of the artist.

In April the family returned to their home on First Mesa so they could plant their corn crop for the season.

Nampeyo returned to Hopi House in February 1907 and again demanded to leave that April, much to the displeasure of the Harvey people, since her pottery demanded a much higher price than that of other Native American artisans. Even the National Museum in Washington D.C. displayed some of her finest work.

The U.S. Land and Irrigation Exposition held in Chicago in 1910 was Nampeyo's last adventure off the reservation. That November, she and Lesou, along with their fourteen-year-old daughter Nellie and her friend Ida Avayo, traveled by wagon to Winslow, where they boarded a train for Chicago. Since they could not fire pots inside the Chicago Coliseum, they took finished earthenware containers with them and demonstrated the art of pottery making to those who flocked to the exposition. Nellie, who spoke English, probably served as interpreter for the entire group, which also consisted of basket makers from Oraibi and Second Mesa.

By this time, Nampeyo was losing her eyesight. Trachoma, an infectious eye disease that results in scarring of the cornea and eventual blindness, is brought on by poor sanitary conditions, lack of water, and an abundance of flies. The infection ran rampant through the Hopi Nation, and the only available treatment was an antiseptic solution that temporarily halted the progression of the disease but did not cure it.

Nampeyo was first treated for the condition sometime between 1890 and 1901, and although her work initially was not affected by the disease, she no longer relied solely on her eyes to paint her distinctive drawings. "When I first began to paint," she said, "I used to go to the ancient village and pick up pieces of pottery and copy the designs. That is how I learned to paint. But now I just close my eyes and see designs and I paint them."

She never fully lost her sight, but the disease eventually left her unable to paint with the skill of her youth. As Nampeyo shaped her pots, Annie added the intricate patterns she had learned by watching her mother. Daughters

Nellie and Fannie followed suit. Even Daisy Hooee, Annie's daughter, learned from Nampeyo. "Everybody painted for her," said Daisy. "Nellie, Fannie and my mother helped her a lot, painted those little fine lines… Her husband, Lesso, he helped—he sure could paint, that old man too." According to Daisy, "Nampeyo had trouble with her voice as well as her eyes, and at a point couldn't talk well, but she could laugh!"

After World War I, tourists flocked to the Hopi reservation. To keep up with the demand for her pottery, Nampeyo produced smaller, plainer vessels and relied on her family to add designs. Yet when Ruth Bunzel interviewed her in 1924, she noted, "Technically, her [Nampeyo's] work is superior to that of any other Hopi potter."

On May 7, 1930, Lesou—farmer, rancher, tanner of hides, maker of moccasins, and Nampeyo's husband for over fifty years—died of influenza and pneumonia.

That July, the first annual Hopi Craftsman Exhibition was held in Flagstaff, run by Mary-Russell Ferrell Colton and her husband, Dr. Harold Sellers Colton, founders of the Museum of Northern Arizona. The purpose of the exhibition was to improve and expose the craftsmanship of Native American artisans to the public. Nampeyo submitted one decorated pot to the exhibition. It sold for $2. She did not enter again until 1934, when she exhibited three pieces she had shaped and formed, but had been painted by Fannie.

In 1890 the U.S. government had built stone houses with red iron roofs below the Hopi mesas, expecting to entice the native people off their towering, yet unsanitary, edifices. The idea did not work, but Nampeyo was given one of these houses. Since she seldom used it, she rented it out to artists, photographers, ethnographers, and anthropologists. Eventually, her son Wesley moved into the red-roofed house in the community named for Tom Polacca. Wesley built a stand at the edge of the road leading to the top of the mesa, so his mother could display and sell her pottery.

On July 20, 1942, Nampeyo died in the red-roofed house below First Mesa. She had continued to shape her pots until about three years before her death. Many say she never lost her vision, but used the eyes of her children and grandchildren to paint the pottery she continued to mold with hands that had never ceased to create exquisite, extraordinary vessels.

MAIE BARTLETT HEARD

[1868~1951]

After Chicago-born Maie Bartlett married Dwight Heard in 1893, the couple headed for California, but only made it as far as Phoenix, where they found the then-small town suited their tastes. Dwight bought the *Arizona Republican* newspaper, and Maie became a traveling librarian, delivering books to rural ranch children.

Maie embraced Arizona's native cultures. She collected Indian pottery, basketry, jewelry, and native costumes. Her rapidly growing collection soon filled every nook and cranny of their home, convincing the Heards to build a museum so others could enjoy their array of indigenous fine art. The museum was almost completed when Dwight died in March 1929. Three months later, Maie opened the doors of the Heard Museum and continued to be the driving force behind its success, adding to the collection with a discerning eye. She knew the origin of every piece of Native American jewelry, basketry, and pottery that entered the museum's doors.

Serving as director, curator, lecturer, and guide for more than twenty years, Maie's philosophy—"to preserve the cultural heritage of those who have so enriched our lives"—is displayed on a small plaque in one of the museum's courtyards.

She also founded the Phoenix Welfare League and was instrumental in obtaining a city library, YWCA gymnasium, land for a civic center, and a building for the Phoenix Little Theater. In 1948 she was named Phoenix Woman of the Year.

The Heard Museum today is one of the nation's most acclaimed institutions of Native American artifacts, history, and culture.

PAINTER WOMAN

Kate Thomson Cory

[1861–1958]

In 1880, the town of Canyon Diablo, situated about halfway between Flagstaff and Winslow, boasted fourteen saloons along Hell Street, ten gambling establishments, four houses of ill repute, and two dance halls. The number of desperados in this boomtown of two thousand cowboys, prospectors, and railroad men, larger and rowdier than nearby Flagstaff, discouraged anyone from pinning on a badge. Yet when diminutive, forty-four-year-old Kate Thomson Cory stepped off the train twenty-five years later, most traces of the hell-raising town were gone. In fact, there was very little to greet her as she forlornly watched the train disappear like a mirage into the desert.

After visiting relatives in Seattle, Washington, in 1905, Kate stopped in Arizona at the invitation of artist Louis Akin, who had regaled her with tales of the beauty of the desert and his desire to start an artist colony on the Hopi reservation. Coming from a privileged family, Kate must have found the starkness of the desert both amazing and terrifying, and she probably never dreamed she would one day be standing in the middle of a desolate, uninhabited wasteland waiting for a ride to an Indian village.

Born February 8, 1861, in Waukegan, Illinois, Kate was one of six children, although only she and a brother survived infancy. Both Abraham Lincoln, before he became president, and Civil War General Ulysses S. Grant occasionally dined at the family home. When her father became a stockbroker in New York City, nineteen-year-old Kate entered the Art Students League of New York, probably the best art school in the nation at the time, and she graduated from Cooper Union for the Advancement of Science and Art (also in New York City) in 1887.

She established herself as a commercial artist in the New York art community and worked as an illustrator for *Recreation* magazine, but seemed eager to explore new surroundings and broaden her artistic vision when she accepted Louis Akin's invitation to visit his proposed site for an artist's colony in Arizona. Only after she realized "that Louis' plan did not bring the party to the reservation and thus I became the 'colony,' " did she decide to stay for a few weeks to sketch and develop new ideas.

Before heading out with trader William Volz and his wife for the two-day, sixty-five-mile buckboard journey to the Hopi reservation, she was invited to visit a nearby Navajo camp.

I had not ridden horseback before, so there was a gathering of the family out in front to see me safely and properly mounted. "Old Roney" was gentle as a cow, but a little restless when one was getting on his back. The thing to do was to mount quickly. One held onto his mane, another stroked his hind quarters, a third patted his nose, while I, according to instructions, and with a sense of vaulting a haystack, grabbed his mane in the left hand, the pommel in the right, and then giving a spring with the one foot in the stirrup and a flying leap with the other, I landed beautifully in the saddle, much to my surprise, but the scornful superiority of the trader's little eight-year-old daughter, who rides with the ease of a circus monkey, held me still quite humble.

"The trip inland to Oraibi," Kate recalled, "was made…in two very blue-sky days and one starry night arriving at our destination just as evening mess was finished."

Her first night was spent below the Hopi mesa at government housing in what she called the "white village." The next day she found a rooftop apartment in the highest house in Oraibi. "You reached it by ladders and little stone steps, and made your peace with the growling dogs on the ascent; but oh! The view when you got there."

She had all of about twenty feet in which to live, and her tiny apartment was filled with leftovers from last year's corn crop. Her landlady, assuring her she would get rid of the ears, opened a trap door and swept the harvest down to the floor below. Unused food particles such as melon and squash seeds, peach pits, and leftover corn were dumped into lower rooms and preserved in ashes, assuring a food supply if a year came when the crops failed and famine threatened.

Her apartment "boasted three fireplaces and a grinding box, and three windows, two rooms, one main one and a small dark one entered by an opening three feet high… I found a little bed spring at another house…braced it in a corner with stones for legs, and with a few sheepskins for mattress, and having found one chair and applied boxes for table and seats, I felt I was really living in the lap of luxury." Her water supply lay six hundred feet below.

The Hopi people were curious about this small, pale woman who had moved into their community. Often, Kate returned to her apartment to find an entire family looking through her papers and belongings while their dinner simmered over one of her fireplaces. Yet they developed a deep fondness for the woman they called "Paina Wurti" (painter woman), and later invited her to become a member of their tribe, but she declined the honor.

During the seven years Kate spent with the Hopis, first at Oraibi on Third Mesa and later at Walpi on First Mesa, she took more than six hundred photographs, considered one of the largest pictorials of the Hopi people as well as one of the most accurate depictions of their culture. They allowed her to view ritualistic ceremonies and invited her into sacred kivas never before visited by outsiders. She documented their daily lives and witnessed life-changing moments such as the ouster of the Hopi faction known as "Hostiles" by the "Friendlies" in 1906, recording the dissidence with her camera. When she lost these negatives, she picked up her paintbrush and reproduced the event in a mural entitled *Migration*, depicting Hostile men, women, and children leaving their Oraibi homes.

Using very unstable nitro-cellulose film, she filtered rainwater to develop her pictures after extracting drowned bugs and rodents from the murky precipitation. The tone of her pictures is extraordinary considering the circumstances under which she developed them.

While using photographs to memorialize events she later painted, Kate also snapped pictures of people going about their daily lives, then recreated these photos in oil, watercolor, pencil, or charcoal. Her eye for detail missed little. While on an outing into the desert, she described "[w]onderful trees...great twisted trunks...limbs that reached out to heaven..." In her journal, which she maintained from July 1909 until December 1910, her artist eye described the rich hues of the desert after a rainstorm: "While I watch & listen to the flood, the distant mesa across the desert, has dyed a deep rich blood color & a long slender span of rain bow has blended into the evening clouds, & the sky west grown radiant & paled."

Photographers today admire Kate Cory's accomplishments under almost primitive conditions and presume she learned much of her talent on the job, since she had no previous training with a camera. Concerned over exploitation of their rituals, Hopi elders placed a ban on all photography in 1917, making Kate's work even more significant.

Her paintings clearly show her admiration and respect for the Hopi people, as she painstakingly recorded meticulous details of ceremonies and costumes. In her rich, multicolored portrait entitled *Hopi Butterfly* or *Butterfly Maiden* (Kate seldom named or dated her paintings, although this painting is signed), a young girl stands with her feet bare. Her whorl hairstyle of large rolled circles over each ear, depicting squash blossoms or butterfly wings, indicates she is of marriageable age. Her feather-like headpiece is made from cottonwood, can weigh as much as

KATE THOMSON CORY

ten pounds, and is held in place with a braid of hair, pulled through a cornhusk ring, which is then tied under her chin. Her black sack dress trimmed in blue is called a manta, and she holds white feathers that represent rain clouds.

Kate also experimented with poetry and prose. She wrote "The Mudheads," "Confessions of a Tomboy," "The Bride," and "Children in Hopi Land," the latter which she wanted to make into a book. She also published the short story, "The Legend of Thumb Butte," about a daydreaming miner. Her descriptive narratives demonstrate her keen eye for color and detail. *The Border* magazine carried her articles depicting life with the Hopi, one of which included a description of the celebrated and sacred Snake Dance.

She learned to communicate with her neighbors and translated more than nine hundred Hopi words and phrases into English with grammatical notes.

Although isolated on the Hopi mesas, Kate maintained connections with the art world. She spent time in Hollywood as a consultant on Western films and had a showing of her paintings at the Kanst Gallery in Los Angeles.

By 1910, however, "life in the Indian country had become too difficult." She began to feel the strain of climbing steep hills and mountainous steps to the mesas. Subsisting under meager conditions took a toll on her health. Yet when she moved to Prescott in 1912, she designed a home that resembled a typical Hopi house, naming it "Oriole."

She had the doors installed upside down to prevent youngsters from reaching the doorknobs, although she had always liked children. Housekeeping was not high on her list of enjoyable tasks, and as a vegetarian, she often ate beans right from the can unless she cooked up something on her wood stove. Unconcerned about money, she often traded her paintings rather than sell them. Wearing rumpled, ragged clothing, townspeople thought her eccentric, although in 1915 *Sunset* magazine named her one of Arizona's most interesting Westerners.

In Prescott, Kate concentrated more on painting than photography, preferring landscapes to people. However, in 1913 she was commissioned to paint the portraits of the president of the Arizona Senate and speaker of the House of Representatives. That same year, she was invited to participate in the Association of American Painters and Sculptors Armory Park Show in New York, which exhibited the works of modern painters such as Vincent Van Gogh and Paul Signac, along with sculptor Alexander Archipenko.

At the beginning of World War I, Kate went back east to work with the Women's Land Army, a group involved with establishing Victory Gardens to support the war effort. While she was there, Standard Aircraft of Newark, New Jersey, employed her to design camouflage patterns for airplane equipment. She also exhibited some of her paintings at New York's Society of Independent Artists.

Back in Prescott after the war, Kate became involved with the Smoki organization, a group of Anglo men dedicated to preserving Native American dances. Her knowledge of Hopi ceremonies was invaluable, and her involvement with the Smoki included working with Arizona historian Sharlot Hall to design the cover for a book Sharlot wrote about the Smoki people. She also designed the cover of Sharlot's book *Cactus and Pine: Songs of the Southwest.* Kate created the Smoki sun symbol emblem and later donated several of her paintings, her journal, and Hopi dictionary to Prescott's Smoki Museum.

In 1929 plans were drawn up to build a dam on the Arizona–Nevada border. Kate picked up her brushes and canvas and set out to record the area before it was flooded. She camped at the site for days, her only companion an old prospector who prepared her food and probably kept her out of harm's way.

Two years later a manufacturing firm hired Kate to create Hopi-inspired wallpaper and china patterns. But when she refused their demands to make changes to her original artwork, the project never materialized.

In 1956, at the age of ninety-five, Kate moved into the Arizona Pioneers Home in Prescott. She died on June 12, 1958.

Kate Cory's prolific portfolio of paintings and photographs illustrates a cultural sensitivity to Hopi rituals and ceremonies, as well as depicting their ordinary daily lives. Her work left a valuable record of the Hopi people, while her own story, *People of the Yellow Dawn,* in which she retold stories from her journal and recalled memories of the Hopi people, remains unpublished.

SANDSTONE SONGS

Katie Lee

[1919–PRESENT]

Born Kathryn Louise Lee in Aledo, Illinois, on October 23, 1919, Katie was only months old when her family moved to the desert east of Tucson. She considers herself "a westerner, born and bred, whether my birth certificate shows it or not," which is probably why she found herself so involved in the saving of one of Arizona's most pristine and beautiful works of nature.

In 1869 explorer John Wesley Powell led the first expedition down the Colorado River into the Grand Canyon. He described the flora and fauna and sought to understand and appreciate the strength and beauty of this magnificent watercourse. Starting at the Green River in Wyoming, Powell and his men spent three months following the mighty Colorado through Utah and into northern Arizona. Coming upon a region he described as having "wonderful features— carved walls, royal arches, glens, alcove gulches, mounds and monuments," he named this impressive site Glen Canyon.

In 1963 Glen Canyon was flooded with millions of acre-feet of water when Glen Canyon Dam was constructed. Protesters fought in vain to stop the drowning of towering ancient edifices and hundreds of tributaries just waiting to be explored. Of all those who vehemently argued against the drowning of Glen Canyon, the voice of Katie Lee, a petite blond actress, singer, songwriter, and author can still be heard cursing the "Wreck the Nation Bureau" (Reclamation Bureau) for ignoring the pleas of weathered river men and women who traversed the blue-green waters of one of nature's most pristine waterways.

"[T]hey covered up 500 temples, churches, music temples," cried Katie, "165 miles of God's creations in forms of churches, alcoves, more alcoves, bridges, you name it, it was all there." She now waits, not always patiently, in her Jerome, Arizona hillside home for nature to return the river to its former self. She knows with all the surety of her ninety-plus years that one day someone else will bathe in the water-filled potholes and sing in the Music Temple recess where her voice once echoed off gigantic sandstone boulders. She has never regretted foregoing a Hollywood career to ride the torrential Colorado River into the spectacular Glen Canyon. This was certainly not the life she envisioned, growing up in Tucson.

Around 1924 the Lee family moved to California, where her father designed some of the first houses lining Los Angeles' Hollywood Hills. However, when the 1929 market crash ruined her father's business, the family returned to Tucson.

Katie and her pals spent most of their waking hours outdoors, exploring nearly every crevice of Sabino Canyon, a natural desert oasis in the Coronado National Forest. "I suppose it was a training ground for what would come later," she wrote. "I learned to stick to near-vertical surfaces; to recognize the temperament of various rock forms; and for sure, what grows beside, on, and especially in between those rocks."

On her thirteenth birthday, her father gave her a .22 Remington rifle and taught her how "to hold it, stand, breathe, sight, aim, allow for drop, and squeeze (not pull) the trigger; then, instructed me in the skinning and gutting of my kill…" Squirrels, rabbits, and quail fell under Katie's deadly aim, and all were greatly appreciated on the Lee dinner table during the Great Depression years.

Despite hard times, Katie's parents saw that she received training in ballet (although it made her dizzy), piano, and drama.

KATIE LEE

"At the age of sixteen I knew I was born to perform. I walked onto a high school stage in the leading role of a play, knowing all my lines and everyone else's, felt those lights hit me (and I was scared shitless standing in the wings) but it was just like walking into my living room. I was at home." In 1942 she graduated from the University of Arizona with a degree in drama and a minor in English. She set her sights on Hollywood.

The onset of World War II, however, changed many lives, including Katie's. She married a soldier, had a son, and was divorced by the time the war ended. She learned to play the guitar, although she still cannot read music. The first tunes she played were Mexican melodies.

In 1948, when one of the directors she had known at Tucson Little Theater, who now worked at the Pasadena Playhouse in Los Angeles, asked her to take a leading role, Katie finally headed for California.

After that, she played a variety of walk-on and character parts in movies and on some of the first television shows including *The Armchair Detective* and *Fireside Theater*. "The trouble was," she said, "I wasn't an ingénue, because I went there in '48, so I had to be twenty-eight years old…too young to be a character actress, and in those days in Hollywood there was nothing in between!"

Eventually acquiring gigs on national radio shows such as *The Great Gildersleeve* (receiving more mail than the star), *The Halls of Ivy* with Ronald Colman, and *The Railroad Hour* with Gordon MacRae, Katie acted, sang, and played the guitar, whatever the roles required. She also sang occasionally in clubs along Hollywood's Sunset Strip.

In 1953 she returned to Tucson to perform at the Temple of Music and Art, receiving rave reviews from the hometown crowd. While at home, she viewed a documentary on a powerboat run through the Grand Canyon, and she knew she had to experience the thrill of this exhilarating, terrifying ride, but could ill afford $500 to traverse the upper half of the river, plus an additional $500 to navigate the lower half. She returned to Hollywood discouraged, not only because she saw no way she could experience this wild adventure but also because "I wanted out of Hollywood. I wanted to get back to my roots, the earth."

She eventually earned her way onto one of the river trips by agreeing to sing for her passage. The trip left her in awe. "I was in shock, literally, like being in a car wreck and coming out unscathed. Nothing of that magnitude had happened to me before. To be on the razor's edge—to know you can die, to see how insignificant you are in relation to time, space, nature, beauty, history, our planet—is to be firmly put in your place. A grain of sand. That's all you are."

Katie became the 175th person to ride down the Colorado River and only the third woman to run all the rapids since Powell's first venture in 1869.

In 1954 she made her first river trip through Glen Canyon and was captivated with the beauty of the sculptures and the allure of ever-changing waterways. She discovered the majesty of formations such as the Music Temple edifice, where her own voice surrounded her and echoed off towering sandstone arches. She reveled in the solitude and contentedly found that few ventured into the tranquil waters and sometimes-unexpected torrents that often tore through the canyon. She never wanted to leave.

Conversely, after six years in Hollywood, Katie wanted out. "I can't stand television, radio is dying, movies give me a pain in the butt, and there ain't no theater."

Folksinger Burl Ives, "a generous man with his time and his good advice," convinced her to take her guitar on the road and sing her songs. She sang in clubs across the country such as the New York's Blue Angel and Downstairs at the Upstairs, and Gate of Horn in Chicago, the most popular folk club in the Midwest. She sang in cafes, coffeehouses, prisons, schools, even old folks' homes. She appeared with television hosts Jack Parr and Dave Garroway. Performing at benefits with Harry Belafonte, she learned to play calypso music from one of his guitarists.

For ten years, Katie stayed on the road. Yet every month she returned to Glen Canyon on the Colorado River, planning the next trip as soon as she got off the last one. "You just can't know how good it felt to take off all my clothes and get back to nature, and feel that water running over my body, and feel the sand pickin' away at my skin, and feel a rock, and getting in step with the stone."

To help her pals who owned the riverboats, she publicized their trips, but soon realized she was going against her own desires. "I really had gotten possessive about the place, and I didn't want anybody else down there anyway—ever."

Since the beginning of her river voyages, Katie had heard of the Bureau of Reclamation's proposal to dam Glen Canyon in order to provide irrigation and hydroelectric power for the western states. Finally, in 1956, President Dwight D. Eisenhower signed into law the Colorado River Storage Project Act authorizing, among other irrigation projects, the damming of Glen Canyon.

Katie passionately opposed the Glen Canyon Dam, inundating Arizona senator Barry Goldwater with letters of protest because he approved the project. She wrote numerous songs demanding Glen Canyon be saved. Yet on October 15, 1956, the first dynamite charges blasted an ugly, disfiguring hole into the walls of the canyon, and the water began to drown the intimate inlets and massive sandstone structures, although it took seven years to fill the giant chasm.

During this time, Katie defied warning signs to keep out and sated her soul with the wonders of Glen Canyon. "I decided to drink until I was drunk with it...because this was going to have to last me the rest of my life—and it has...

I can see practically every turn in that river. I can still see the sandbars and feel it all." She sang her last song in Music Temple in 1962, the year before the diversion tunnels were closed and the Colorado River started filling what would become Lake Powell.

Katie left Arizona for seven years, singing to skiers in Aspen, Colorado. In 1964 she recorded *The Folk Songs and Poems of the Colorado River,* one more protest against the damming of Glen Canyon.

She returned to Arizona and settled in Sedona in 1969. Two years later, she embarked on a nine-month stint traveling through thirty-six states and 147 towns, singing with the National Humanities Series.

She moved to the small mining community of Jerome, settling into a bright blue house that bears a sign above the door requesting all to "Sing." Today, she still cries when she talks of the loss of Glen Canyon and the wonders she first envisioned over fifty years ago.

Katie receives countless letters praising her fight to restore the majestic abyss. One young woman wrote she could not "image the heartbreak of losing something as treasured as Glen Canyon…" and promised to use her youth and energy to keep fighting for its return.

It is the children who truly understand Katie's quest. "When I do my readings and songs at grade schools, where the students are between ages thirteen to fifteen, I am overwhelmed by their interest, participation, and awe."

She continues the fight. In 1998 she wrote *All My Rivers Are Gone,* republished in 2006 as *Glen Canyon Betrayed—A Sensuous Elegy,* describing the death of her beloved Glen Canyon. *Sandstone Seduction* was published in 2004.

Her first book, *Ten Thousand Goddam Cattle,* contains a history of the cowboy in song, story, and verse. In conjunction with the book, she produced a television documentary, *The Last Wagon,* commemorating the lives of Arizona cowboy legends Gail Gardner and Billy Simon, which won the Cline Golden Eagle Award in 1972. She was also featured on the PBS series *Cadillac Desert.* Recording more than a dozen albums and CDs, her latest endeavor, a DVD titled *Love Song to the Glen Canyon,* depicts the loss of the canyon in photographs and song.

She serves on the advisory Board of the Glen Canyon Institute, a nonprofit organization advocating the draining and restoration of the canyon.

Katie is well aware of the loss to the Grand Canyon by the damming of Glen Canyon. "The biodiversity is what saves the life of a river and Glen Canyon saved the life of the Grand. The Grand Canyon is dying on its feet. It's a mess. It's a slimy, cold, unnatural, completely rearranged ecology down there. The biodiversity is shot. And it's a bloody sin."

She is not yet ready to quit.

WOMEN OF THE LAW

A rizona's first territorial legislature met in Prescott in the fall of 1864. That December, the Territorial Supreme Court admitted seven men to practice law within its boundaries. Not until Sarah Sorin applied in 1892 did women enter Arizona's legal profession. Sarah scaled heights beyond Arizona's borders in 1913, when she became the first woman to argue a case before the U.S. Supreme Court without a male attorney at her side.

Women were active in politics years before they took to the bench or ran for office. They served on boards and committees establishing educational and health-care reform and fought for social welfare and religious freedom. Without women involved in charitable organizations, thousands would have gone hungry; women and children would have been left in abusive situations with nowhere to turn. The country did not recognize these activities as political, but many of these associations today are deeply involved in the political process.

The impact of women in the law was especially prevalent during Arizona's early development and progress. Some of this success can be traced to Native American women such as Yavapai chieftess Viola Jimulla, who ran the Prescott Yavapai tribe for more than twenty years, passing the leadership on to her daughters and granddaughters. Annie Wauneka represented her people on the Navajo Tribal Council for just as many years, fighting for better health care and living conditions. Without her determination and fortitude, the spread of disease across the Navajo Reservation would have devastated the entire populace.

Schoolteacher, and riverboat and airplane pilot, Nellie Bush walked into the Arizona House of Representatives in 1920 and stayed for the next fourteen years. And Lorna Lockwood paved a path for others to follow when she became the first woman chief justice of the Arizona Supreme Court.

So many followed in the footsteps of Arizona's first women attorneys and politicians, such as longtime legislator and centenarian Polly Rosenbaum;

[153]

congresswoman Isabella Greenway; gubernatorial candidate Ana Frohmiller; Phoenix mayor Margaret Hance; governors Rose Mofford, Jane Hull, Janet Napolitano, and Jan Brewer; and of course, the first woman to sit on the U.S. Supreme Court, Arizona's own Sandra Day O'Connor. The legal and political future of Arizona is in excellent hands.

SOLO PERFORMANCE

Sarah Inslee Herring Sorin
[1861–1914]

The likelihood of a woman arguing a case on her own before the U.S. Supreme Court in the early 1900s was highly improbable. Women attorneys had appeared in the highest court of the land, but only as assistants to male litigators. Women were thought not to have the reasoning or judgment necessary to plead difficult cases, and many believed the "delicate sex" did not have the constitution to stand up to the rigors of court proceedings. When Sarah Sorin stood before the esteemed council of nine Supreme Court judges and argued her case in 1913, she proved women capable of entering the legal profession on all levels and in their own stead, even if they did not yet have the right to vote.

Sarah was an unlikely candidate to become the first women to argue a case solely on her own before the U.S. Supreme Court. Born in New York City on January 5, 1861, Sarah Inslee Herring, the oldest of William and Mary Herring's five children, taught school until the family moved west and settled in the raucous mining town of Tombstone in 1882, shortly after the infamous Earp brothers' shootout on the town's notorious blood-soaked streets.

William Herring was a prominent local attorney in the rough, tough town and occasionally found himself involved in legal matters with Wyatt Earp. According to one Herring descendent, in January 1882, as William prepared to escort Wyatt and his cohorts out of Tombstone, twenty-one-year-old Sarah insisted on riding with her father. Of course William had no intention of allowing his daughter to be part of such a dangerous situation, but Sarah had always been a strong-willed young woman, used to getting her way. She informed her father she would follow behind if forbidden to ride with him. Knowing the determination of his eldest and supposedly favorite daughter, William relented. Sarah rode with her father and the Earp entourage without incident.

William Herring was also a delegate to the 1891 Constitutional Convention and served as Arizona territorial attorney general (1892–1893). His only son, Howard, practiced law with him, while daughter Bertha worked in the office as stenographer, notary, and overseer of probate cases.

Sarah continued her teaching career in Tombstone, becoming one of the town's first female educators. She also held the position of librarian and reportedly became the first female school principal in the territory.

In 1891 Sarah's brother Howard met an untimely death from a lethal dose of cocaine administered by the local dentist. In an effort to help her father, Sarah resigned from teaching to study law under his tutelage. After an examination on November 24, 1892, in the First Judicial District Court of the Territory of Arizona, newspapers reported that "Miss Herring answered all questions propounded in an intellectual manner…" The test was a "most rigid examination, which she passed with the most distinguished honors." With no resistance or argument, Sarah became the first female attorney in Arizona Territory.

Two months later, she was admitted to practice before the Arizona Supreme Court. The *Arizona Weekly Star* reported her accomplishments as "blazing a path for women in Arizona to higher and wider fields for the exercise of their talent. She has asserted her divine right to use the brain, courage, and energy given her. She has thrown down the gauntlet to the so-called sterner sex, in asserting the right of woman to enter the race of life on equal terms with man. It was a courageous step, taken by a courageous lady, and henceforth many other of our young women will follow in her path."

To further her legal education, she enrolled in New York University's School of Law, graduating with honors in 1894. Returning to Tombstone, she hung her shingle next to her father's in the law firm of Herring & Herring. She specialized in mining law, although she and her father also handled criminal cases and divorces—issues unfit for a woman to hear, according to her male counterparts. In addition, she took on other legal matters such as guardianships, probates, land grant claims, corporate issues, and accident cases.

The latter issue first took Sarah before the Arizona Territorial Supreme Court in 1896. Michael Welch had won a judgment in district court against his employers, G. W. Seaverns and Quincy A. Shaw. The Herring law firm represented the employers. Sarah appealed the decision, and her closing argument convinced the judge to reverse the lower court's finding and remand the case for a new trial.

Learned male colleagues in the courtroom that day described Sarah's demeanor as cool under pressure, noting she was thoroughly prepared. "The judge listened most attentively, and not one in the audience permitted his attention to flag." One lawyer even admitted that the new lady lawyer had "excelled him in argument," as she did with many of his colleagues.

In 1895 Herring & Herring represented the Copper Queen Consolidated Mining Company against the U.S. government in a lengthy case disputing whether lands where timber was cut were mineral lands. William Herring argued before the U.S. Supreme Court in 1902, but Sarah's early participation was duly noted in the *Bisbee Review*. "The Queen company won a clean victory over the big United States and much of the credit is due to the fine legal ability of this eminent lady."

After successful cases representing major mining operations in Globe and Bisbee, Herring & Herring felt the need to relocate. In 1897, with mines failing and flooding, Tombstone was becoming a dying town. The Herring family moved to Tucson and reopened the doors of the father/daughter law firm.

Moving to Tucson was not the only major change for Sarah during the ensuing year. On July 21, 1898, thirty-seven-year-old Sarah married fifty-two-year-old Thomas Robertson Sorin, a rancher in the Dragoon Mountains. Sorin also owned several copper mines in the area and was co-founder of the *Tombstone Epitaph*, along with Indian agent and former Tombstone mayor John Clum.

The wedding was held in the Herrings' Tucson home, with the parlors "tastily decorated with flowers and evergreens, and the very atmosphere seemed to breathe of loveliness," according to the *Tucson Daily Star*.

Changing the firm's name to Herring & Sorin, Sarah stayed in Tucson during the workweek, returning to Thomas's Dragoon ranch on weekends. An avid rider, she enjoyed the freedom of the countryside after a strenuous week of legal maneuvering. "Without a daily canter on my good horse my spirits and energies would fail entirely," she once remarked. "It is the best tonic a woman can take."

Frontier law suited Sarah's strong, resolute character. Raising a family, however, proved unattainable after their first and only child was stillborn.

Sarah's skills in the courtroom often made the newspapers. A 1903 *Tombstone Epitaph* article commented: "Mrs. Sorin is at perfect ease in a courtroom and commands the respect of both judge and jury and wins the admiration of the bar for the graceful manner in which she handles her case; she is never at a loss for authorities, being so thoroughly prepared as to have references at her fingers' end, and no matter how complicated the issue, she possesses that happy facility of elucidation that most generally wins for her client a favorable verdict..."

On April 16, 1906, William Herring submitted a motion to admit Sarah to practice before the U.S. Supreme Court. When she took the oath of office, easterner Belva Lockwood, the first woman so honored, proudly looked on.

Oddly enough, for a woman of such remarkable courage and fortitude, Sarah was not an advocate for women's suffrage. In an interview the day of her

SARAH INSLEE HERRING SORIN

admission to the U.S. Supreme Court, she was asked about her stand on women's right to vote. She admitted she had never "advocated giving the ballot to women, for I have never wanted to vote myself. It seems to me that men ought to be trusted to run the affairs of this nation, and it is extremely doubtful whether extending the suffrage to women would result in any good." She had once been asked to run for district attorney of Cochise County, but refused the offer.

That October, Sarah appeared with her father before the august body in her first U.S. Supreme Court case. The firm of Herring & Sorin won a favorable opinion. She followed the next year with another appearance alongside her father, but Justice Oliver Wendell Holmes delivered an opinion against the Tucson law firm.

In 1912 Sarah's father died. She dissolved the Herring & Sorin law firm and moved her practice to Globe, Arizona, becoming counsel for Old Dominion Copper Company and United Globe Mines. She again went to Washington D.C. to stand beside her brother-in-law, attorney Selim M. Franklin, who was presenting a Supreme Court action.

Sarah's fourth appearance before the U.S. Supreme Court occurred on November 6, 1913. No man stood beside her as she argued the points in a case pitting United Globe Mines against James Work in a quiet title action on the O'Daugherty and Big Johnny Mines. Sarah and her father started this case in 1906, and it had made its way through the courts during the ensuing years. Now, without her father, she stood alone to fight her client's position.

"Arizona Woman Lawyer First to Appear Before Supreme Court at Washington as Sole Representative," read the headline in the *Tombstone Prospector*. The article declared Sarah "the sole pleader for the defending claim in behalf of the United Globe Mines… Mrs. Sorin fought the case through the Arizona Supreme Court, where a decision was rendered in her favor."

Her argument was "one of the most brilliant ever presented to that court by a woman," proclaimed the *Women Lawyers Journal* in later years. The decision handed down on January 4, 1914, was in favor of United Globe Mines.

Sarah was forging a great legal career. Four months later, however, fifty-three-year-old Sarah died. Her death certificate listed the cause of death as pneumonia as a result of influenza. Her career as an intelligent and compassionate advocate for her clients' interests stopped at the imposing doors of the U.S. Supreme Court.

To honor his wife, Thomas printed a small booklet containing a portrait of Sarah and including two of her poems. Sarah wrote "Glimpses of Arizona" shortly after arriving in the West and "God's Sunshine" after her brother's death. Thomas decorated the booklet with juniper branches, her favorite plant. He also had a juniper branch carved on her gravestone.

Tucson attorneys came en masse to her funeral. The Arizona State Bar Association recorded a special resolution extolling Sarah's integrity and ability. "[A]s a woman she was the embodiment of all those noble qualities of life which have been the admiration of the civilized world... [H]er moral conception of duty, her reverence for the ethics of her profession and her constant and consistent adherence to principles of fairness and honor place her high in the regard of her associates... [T]he bar of this state is deprived of one of its most brilliant and most eminent members and one whose place can never be filled."

In 1985 Sarah was inducted into the Arizona Women's Hall of Fame. In 1999 the Arizona Women Lawyers Association created the annual Sarah Sorin Award, given "to an Arizona Women Lawyers Association member who has demonstrated support and encouragement for the advancement of women in the legal profession." She was listed as one of Arizona's top 100 women and minority lawyers in 2000.

Sarah Sorin paved the way for future generations of women to appear before the U.S. Supreme Court with full confidence that their arguments would carry as much weight as those of their male counterparts. She was confident and skilled in her abilities as an attorney. Had she lived longer, who knows what other barriers she might have conquered.

CHIEFTESS

Sicatuva (Viola Pelhame Jimulla)
[1878–1966]

The San Carlos Apache Indian Reservation was established in 1871 to maintain control over Apache warriors and their families. Disease, pollution, and snakes were mainstays of reservation life, along with sometimes-brutal treatment at the hands of Indian agents. In February 1875 approximately 1,500 Yavapai and Tonto Apaches were forced-marched to San Carlos from the Camp Verde Indian Reservation, a two-hundred-mile trek known as the "March of Tears." One young girl who survived the ordeal remembered vividly walking where "[t]here was no road, and very few trails. Many had no moccasins, but those who did gave them to others who needed them more. Even the moccasins wore out on the sharp rocks. Our clothing was torn to rags on the brush and cactus. With bleeding feet, weary in body and sick at heart, many wanted to die. Many did die."

SICATUVA (VIOLA PELHAME JIMULLA)

More than one hundred did not survive the two-week march across the freezing wilderness. Two Yavapai who did endure were Woo-wah (Singing Cricket) and Ka-hava-soo-ah (Turquoise). Three years later, Sicatuva (Born Quickly) was born to this couple, probably in the early summer, as she eventually chose June 15, 1878, for her birth date.

Like most Yavapai children, Sicatuva ran across the reservation in her bare feet, wearing scant clothing. "I always hated the feeling of wet mud oozing between my toes," she later recalled, "and when I came to a creek bank, I would stop and stand still and cry, and would not cross."

Around age fifteen, Sicatuva attended the Indian day school at nearby Rice, Arizona. By this time her father had died and her mother had remarried a man named Pelhame. Sicatuva enrolled in school as Viola Pelhame. She went on to Phoenix Indian School for about five years, learning the refinements of cooking and sewing while improving her mastery of the English language and gaining an understanding of Christianity.

While Viola was at school, her mother and stepfather were allowed to leave the reservation, settling on land around Fort Whipple, near present-day Prescott. Viola visited her mother in 1900 and chose to stay in the Prescott area rather than return to school. She found work cooking at the Blue Bell Mine near Mayer, a mining town a few miles away.

The following year she married Sam Jimulla, who had also been born on the San Carlos Reservation. They had five daughters, although two of them died in infancy. Daisy was born in July 1902, living only seven months. Grace arrived in November 1903, followed by Lucy in June 1906. Amy was born in October 1912, but died two years before her thirtieth birthday. In September 1913 Rosie was born. She passed away about a year later.

Life was difficult for the Jimulla family during these times, but both Sam and Viola thrived on hard work. Viola had no trouble finding employment cleaning homes in the Prescott area. When Sam's work took him out of the area, however, or when he went hunting, she usually accompanied him. Grace, Lucy, and Amy all attended Phoenix Indian School.

In 1872 a Yavapai Indian mission was established in the Prescott area. It was rarely active until 1922, when a small building run by the Presbyterian Church served the Yavapai people. Every other Sunday, the minister from Clarkdale attended to the congregation, relying on Sam and Viola to act as interpreters and elders of the church. Viola also became Sunday school superintendent.

Although she first learned about Christianity during her school years, it was not until she returned to Prescott that Viola became a Christian. "Occasionally some members of the Salvation Army would come to the reservation for outdoor meetings," she said, "and I heard through them that God loved me and would forgive me for my sins and I wanted to try Him." Viola became the first Yavapai baptized in the Presbyterian Church.

"It wasn't easy, because the other Indians used to make fun of me. When they see me on the trail to town, they would look out of their houses and holler to the others to look out and see a Christian Indian, and they would laugh."

She continued to be active in the Presbyterian Church the rest of her life. With others, she revitalized the Yavapai Indian Mission and helped to form the Trinity Presbyterian Church for the Yavapai people. Viola represented the congregation at the Southwest Missionary Conference held in Flagstaff in 1938 and again in 1940. She was a delegate to a meeting in Albuquerque, New Mexico, consisting of Indians from fourteen different tribes. In 1946 she was instrumental in organizing the first Indian Camp Meeting held by the Presbyterian Church, and in 1950 she served as commissioner to the General Assembly of the United Presbyterian Church in Cincinnati, Ohio.

In the early 1930s, Viola and Sam, along with prominent Prescott pioneers, were instrumental in obtaining seventy-five acres of land recognized by the U.S. Senate as the Yavapai–Prescott Indian Reservation, one of the smallest reservations in the country. The Bureau of Indian Affairs appointed Sam as chief of the Yavapai–Prescott tribe. Later, he was officially elected chief by his people.

Sam headed a Civil Works Administration project to build more substantial housing for the Yavapai using native granite, stone, and concrete. He postponed the construction of his own home until the end of the project, but money ran out before the Jimulla residence could be completed. Contributions from their own people allowed the family to finish their own dwelling.

On March 12, 1940, Amy Jimulla died, leaving four young children. Gathering up her grandchildren, Viola took them into her home and raised them to adulthood.

Tragedy struck again just two months later, when Sam was thrown from his horse. He died on May 21. Because of her education and involvement in the community and church, Viola became the logical choice to take his place, assuming the title of chieftess of the Yavapai–Prescott tribe.

While Sam previously went about his responsibilities with quiet dignity, Viola grabbed the reins of her duties and set off to improve the lives of her people. "We do not want anything fancy," she said. "No fine homes, nor much land. All we want is equal opportunity and the right to take our place as full-fledged Americans." She was instrumental in establishing the Prescott Tribal Council that same year, overseeing and approving issues that affected the welfare of the tribe.

For twenty-six years, Viola worked to acquire better living conditions, more modern facilities, and education for the Yavapai people. She agreed to withdraw tribal claims to land grants at old Fort Whipple in exchange for a community college and park built on the property. The Prescott campus of Yavapai College now stands on this site.

Over the years, Viola and Sam had tried without success to acquire additional land for the Yavapai-Prescott Reservation, but were told repeatedly that adding more Indian land would interfere with the public domain of Prescott's Anglo citizens. Finally, in the early 1950s, the reservation expanded from about 75 acres to 1,327.

Viola served as interpreter for court cases involving non-English-speaking Yavapai. When asked to speak about the history and culture of her people, she never hesitated, knowing that knowledge would bring understanding. Organizations such as the Yavapai County Archaeological Society and the Yavapai Gem and Mineral Society, recognizing her talents as a spokeswoman for her people, elected her an honorary life member.

In 1951 the Yavapai chieftess took on an obligation far beyond normal expectations for her seventy-three years, serving as counselor for thirty schoolchildren on a four-day camping trip through Yosemite National Park, plus a week-long sightseeing tour of San Francisco. For many of these children from five different tribes, this excursion took them off the reservation for the first time. Their lives would evolve in a different world than that of Viola's upbringing.

As a child on the San Carlos Reservation, Viola wove her first basket under the tutelage of her mother. As was custom, she took her small basket to the finest basketmaker among her people for her blessing. Viola went on to become one of the preeminent basket weavers among the Yavapai, teaching others as her mother had taught her. As she worked alongside Apache basket weavers at San Carlos, techniques from both tribes intermingled and melded into unique shapes and designs. The symbol on the Yavapai-Prescott Indian Tribal flag is derived from one of Viola's woven designs.

Viola died on December 7, 1966. Her daughter Grace Jimulla Mitchell succeeded her as chieftess, and later her other daughter, Lucy Jimulla Miller, filled those dusty, history-laden shoes. Her granddaughter Patricia McGee also served as president of the Yavapai-Prescott tribe.

Longtime friend Arizona senator Barry Goldwater remembered Viola shortly after her death. "To me," he said, "Viola was never an old person; she was forever young...endowed with a calmness of heart and kind to all... Viola was one of those rare people whose walk down the pathway of life raised a fine dust, which falling on those who travel the trail at the same time was beneficial to them. She was generous of heart and kind to all."

THE BEST "MAN" IN THE RACE

Nellie May Trent Bush

[1888–1963]

When Nellie May Trent's family first moved to Mesa, Arizona, in 1893, they lived in a tent. The five-year-old worked alongside her mother washing other people's clothes, shelling almonds in a nearby factory, and wearing dresses made from flour sacks. In school she excelled, completing her studies at age fourteen. To earn her way through Tempe Normal School (now Arizona State University), she milked cows before she went to class. From these humble beginnings, Nellie worked to improve the lives of every Arizona man, woman, and child. Undaunted by any task, she taught school, ran a hotel, started a water company and electric utility, piloted her own riverboat and airplane, organized women's clubs around the state, and climbed one political ladder after another.

Born November 29, 1888, in Cedar County, Missouri, Nellie learned early in life to shape her own destiny. After earning a teaching certificate from Tempe Normal School in 1908, she taught in Mesa and Glendale before marrying trolley car conductor Joseph Everett Bush on Christmas Day 1912.

In 1915 Joe bought an interest in a ferryboat business along the Colorado River, shepherding passengers and freight up and down the river from the small community of Parker, Arizona. Nellie, six months pregnant, arrived in Parker in the middle of a sandstorm and was completely overwhelmed with the elements and the grand total of thirty-five people who called this godforsaken place home. There were no paved roads, no electricity or running water, and only one telephone line for the entire town. She "sat down under a greasewood tree and cried," then dried her eyes and boarded the boat that would become her home.

Life was not easy along the muddy embankment of the Colorado River. When she was due to give birth, she pawned her wedding ring to afford the train ride to Phoenix. Wesley Bush was born on September 11, 1915.

With another mouth to feed, Nellie was soon teaching and acting as principal at the small Parker school. She was elected to the Parker School Board in 1916, her initiation into the political arena. She and Joe ran Parker's Cut-Off Hotel before building the Grandview Hotel in 1917. To lure people to the Grandview, they squandered $25 on a Model T Ford bereft of its top and windshield. Nellie drove down dirt roads posting signs advertising the small lodge, frequently stopping to fix a flat tire. Once, when the engine died and she discovered a broken timing spring, she plucked a wire spring from her corset, fixed the engine, and drove on down the road.

It was the ferryboat and the unpredictable Colorado River, however, which occasionally brought Nellie to her knees.

Life aboard the *Nellie T* was fraught with danger as Nellie and Joe hauled ore down the river to waiting freights trains in Parker. "Waves sometimes would be over eight feet high," she said. "Often when we were caught on the river in a storm, we'd have to throw overboard some of the ore. Many a time when the sailing was dangerous and I thought about my baby in the pilot house, I've uttered a little prayer, 'Now if you'll just let me get this kid off of here alive, I'll never bring him back on board again.' But you forgot about that after the danger had passed."

The little steamer could handle about twenty tons of copper, gold, or manganese, or carry six automobiles across the sometimes-tempestuous waterway. In 1920 Nellie obtained the first riverboat license issued to a woman in the United States.

By now she was also serving as Parker's justice of the peace. Feeling that she did not have the background for a political career, she took a correspondence course in law, which held her in good stead when she was elected Yuma County delegate to the Arizona House of Representatives in 1920. She firmly believed "women must live and raise families under the laws of the state, therefore they must protect that sphere in which they move. That is woman's reason for being in politics."

When asked if she felt it appropriate to be away from her family while serving in the legislature, she retorted, "I have a husband and a big five-year-old son, yet I do not feel that they are being neglected because of my work. My folks take good care of the boy while I'm here, and my husband is right back of me in my public career."

The following year she and six-year-old Wesley moved to Tucson when Nellie entered law school at the University of Arizona "We would part each morning, my son going one way and I the other. He used to tell people, 'Mother and I are both in the first grade.'"

Nellie and future Arizona chief justice Lorna Lockwood were the first two women to enroll in the university's law school. Determining that their delicate constitutions could not bear to hear such traumatizing issues as rape cases, the professor sent his two female students from the classroom when this subject arose. Nellie handled the dismissal with her usual aplomb, asking the professor if he "had ever heard of a rape case that didn't involve a woman. They let us in after that."

When her duties in the legislature interfered with her schoolwork, she attended summer classes at the University of California, Berkeley. She never graduated from the University of Arizona School of Law, but was admitted to practice in Arizona in 1923 and in California in 1927. Finishing her term in the legislature, she opened her law practice in Parker and counted the City of Parker and the Southern Pacific Railroad among her clients.

Early in her political career, Nellie introduced a House bill that would allow women to serve on juries, but it died before gaining support. Women would not obtain the right to serve on Arizona juries until 1945.

In 1926 she ran for office again and was elected to serve Yuma County in the Arizona House of Representatives, becoming the first woman to chair the prestigious Judiciary Committee. She proposed a bill to create a home for mentally challenged children, and over Governor George W. P. Hunt's veto, she was successful in establishing the Children's Colony near Coolidge, Arizona.

Nellie and Governor Hunt often faced off across the aisle, even though they were both Democrats. "I never considered myself 'his person', " she once remarked, "and when it was necessary I stood up to be counted against him."

She served on a joint Senate and House committee that investigated the Highway Department, which was found to be the governor's personal political machine. The *Los Angeles Times* called her a "thorn in the side of Gov. Hunt," and she knew he threatened to "get me out of the Legislature one way or another." She lost her bid for the Arizona Senate in 1928, but returned to the House in 1930.

In 1931 Nellie sponsored a bill to erect a bridge across the Colorado River at Parker, a move that would close down the ferry business. One legislator, noting he had ridden on Nellie and Joe's ferry "admir[ed] her for coming and fighting for her people at her own expense and therefore I am going to vote for her bill."

"There was thunderous applause," wrote one reporter, "and again when it was announced that the bill had passed."

However, when a bill to enhance vocational training was turned down as costing more than the state could afford, Nellie offered, "They have just voted me $75,000 for my bridge, but something for the children is more important. If we can't have both, I'll give up the bridge."

In 1931 teenager Wesley expressed an avid interest in aviation. Both he and Nellie went back to school to earn their pilots' licenses and to build Parker's first airfield. After that, Nellie took to the skies whenever she hit the campaign trail.

She attended the Democratic National Convention held in Chicago in 1932 with full expectation of nominating her friend and Arizona congresswoman Isabella Greenway as a vice presidential candidate, but was disappointed when support was thrown to John Nance Garner. "I think it's

NELLIE MAY TRENT BUSH

just too bad that at least one woman won't get the honor of being mentioned at this convention," she complained.

In 1934 Nellie was successful in her bid for a seat in the Arizona Senate, even though controversy again followed her into chambers as storm clouds hovered over the Colorado River. Serving on the Arizona Colorado River Water Commission and later as a member of the Colorado River Basin States Committee, she was smack in the middle of controversy when Governor Benjamin B. Moeur, objecting to California wanting more than its share of river water, proclaimed martial law along Arizona's shores and recruited Nellie and Joe's steamers to ferry National Guard troops across the river to halt construction of Parker Dam. The media exploded with news of a war between the two states. A photograph of Nellie at the helm of one of the boats appeared in newspapers across the country, and she was dubbed "Admiral of the Arizona Navy."

Isabella Greenway announced her retirement from the U.S. Congress in 1936. Nellie almost immediately announced her candidacy for the seat. "If you send me to Congress," she promised, "I will go as the representative of all the people of the state of Arizona and... I will be under no obligation to any person, corporation or faction."

"Vote for Nellie T. Bush, the best 'man' in the race for Congress," proclaimed her campaign signs. Losing in the Democratic primary, Nellie returned to the Arizona House of Representatives in 1940.

She had been active in women's organizations since teaching school in Glendale, where she organized the Glendale Women's Club (and later, in Parker, the Parker Women's Club). Her colleagues in the Arizona Business and Professional Women's Association had unsuccessfully lobbied to have her named Speaker of the House in 1941. She also served as president of the Arizona Federation of Women's Clubs in 1955.

A woman of many talents, Nellie took up painting in the late 1930s, with one of her more noted works a portrayal of the "Arizona Navy" she commanded on the Colorado River in 1934, depicting the *Nellie T, Nellie Jo,* and *Julia B.* sailing off to defend Arizona's coastline.

Always ready for a good debate, she once wrote to President John F. Kennedy, chastising him for calling American businessmen SOBs.

My good old father was in the business of farming and, as the oldest child of the family, I helped him plant seeds, grain, alfalfa, melons and the like and in due time worked hard in the fields harvesting the crops, not only to provide eats for our own family but for others who were in other businesses besides raising foods... I worked just as hard...during World

War I, bringing copper and manganese ores from the hills down the Colorado River by boat to the Santa Fe Railway for shipping… [We] built a water works and light plant in the little town of Parker and ran these plants so the people could have water and lights… But, Mr. President: I never thought I'd see the day when I would be told by the son-of-a-liquor-man that I was a son of a bitch for the humble efforts I had made in behalf of my country.

Nellie died on October 27, 1963, still serving the people of Parker as a member of the city council. She won more elections than she lost but was not above admitting her defeats. As she liked to say, "I always bounced back."

"EVERYBODY WALKS WITH YOU"

Annie Dodge Wauneka
[1910–1997]

When I went to elementary school on the reservation, the speaking of Navajo in or at the school was forbidden. And when I went to high school at the Albuquerque Indian School, the speaking of Navajo was still prohibited. So I and many of my Pueblo friends decided that we were going to speak the very best English that we could. It was very unfortunate that I had to forsake my Navajo friends and not enjoy the privilege of speaking my native language. But it probably turned out better this way."

The decision by young Annie Dodge to become proficient in the English language did have a fortunate outcome. From the time she left school in the eleventh grade, she followed in her father's footsteps as arbitrator and advocate for the Navajo people. Her ability to communicate with Anglo administrators, even U.S. congressmen, gave her power within her community and the ability to foster understanding between the two cultures. Few Navajo women have risen to the heights attained by this little shepherd girl who understood the problems facing her tribe and strived to enlighten her people.

Annie was born on the Navajo Reservation on April 11, 1910. Her mother Kee'hanabah was a wife of Henry Chee Dodge, one of the wealthiest and most respected Navajo ranchers and leaders. When she was about a year old, Chee

ANNIE DODGE WAUNEKA

Dodge took her to his ranch at Sonsola Buttes near Crystal, New Mexico, and gave her to Nanabah, another of his wives. Not until Nanabah died in 1939 was Annie told that Kee'hanabah was her birth mother.

At age five, Annie started herding small bands of sheep, a typical chore for young Navajo children. In 1918, her father sent the eight-year-old to a government boarding school at Fort Defiance, just as the Spanish influenza epidemic hit the Navajo Reservation with a vengeance. Within days, hundreds of children and most of the school staff were stricken with the disease, including Annie. She was fortunate though and only caught a mild case. With one nurse to care for everyone, the little girl was called on to clean and fill kerosene lanterns so there would be light at night to tend to the bedridden and count the dead.

Across the reservation, more than two thousand people died from the scourge, mostly the healthy and strong rather than the young, old, and infirm.

When school closed in the spring, Annie returned home to Sonsola Buttes for lambing season, as she did every year during her school days.

She completed fifth grade at Fort Defiance and went on to Albuquerque Indian School. An excellent student, she usually completed two grades each year.

In 1923 Henry Chee Dodge, who had learned to speak English at an early age and was employed by the U.S. government as an interpreter, became the first chairman of the newly organized Navajo Tribal Council. Chee Dodge played an integral role in resolving disputes between the Navajos and government agents, and believed education was the key to bringing his people into the twentieth century.

By the time Annie left school in 1928, Chee Dodge owned two large ranches— his home at Sonsola Buttes, where Annie was raised, and another large spread at Tanner Springs south of Ganado, Arizona. In 1929 Annie married George Wauneka, a young man she had met at school. The couple ran the Tanner Springs ranch, adding ten children to the family, losing one in infancy.

"My mother used to cook prairie dogs and make them taste so good," recalled daughter Irma. "My father would catch four or five prairie dogs, and my mother cleaned them on the inside and took off most of their hair by singeing them over a fire. Then she stuffed them with plants and herbs and closed them with baling wire. When the fire in the ground had burned down, she'd lay the prairie dogs side by side over the coals, cover them, and let them bake. That was my favorite meal as a child."

However, Annie spent little time at home. Her father relied on her to attend meetings with him and assist with interpreting. George became caretaker of their children, several of whom had disabilities from difficult births.

By nature Annie was shy and seldom spoke at meetings. When she mentioned a discrepancy to her father after a gathering, he chastised her for her lack of fortitude. Devoted to her father, Annie learned to express her opinions and eventually gained the respect of council members.

She defiantly found her voice when government officials, in a quest to reduce the number of livestock on the reservation, insisted on taking the only horse belonging to an old woman. As the horse was led into the corral, Annie boldly returned it to the woman, much to the consternation of one of the men. He seized the rope and struggled with Annie. "[A]ll of a sudden, I jerked this rope out of his hand and whipped the horse with it and the horse took off running. And I said, 'Okay, gentlemen, go get that horse.' " Annie argued the old lady would probably die soon and should be allowed to keep the horse. The woman lived thirty more years to the age of 110.

As she became a dominant figure at tribal meetings, Annie worked with her father to improve living conditions on the reservation. Chee Dodge wanted more boarding schools and advocated the teaching of English to Navajo children. He fought to stop the sale of liquor to Indians, knowing its effect on his people. Ninety-year-old Henry Chee Dodge died on January 7, 1947, leaving Annie to continue in his stead.

In 1951 she was elected to the Tribal Council, only the second woman to hold a seat on the council. The following year she went to Washington D.C. to represent the Navajo Nation. This was the first of many trips she made across the country to speak for her people in the Nation's capital.

In 1953 she was appointed chair of the Health and Welfare Division of the Community Services Committee that dealt with the issue of tuberculosis on the reservation. The U.S. surgeon general appointed her to the Advisory Committee on Indian Health in 1956.

Annie was keenly aware of the ravages tuberculosis wrought on her people. In order to fight this debilitating and deadly disease, she sought out experts to better understand the sickness. She took classes at the University of Arizona and received a degree in public health.

She visited hogans and witnessed firsthand the toll contagious diseases took on families. She discovered many had received treatment, but upon returning home, they fell into old patterns of poor nutrition and unsanitary living conditions. She encouraged medicine men and doctors to work together to provide understanding of medical issues.

Annie taught her people how to improve their health by explaining that a disease would return if they did not adopt a healthier lifestyle. She tore across the reservation in her beat-up old station wagon, and later an equally disheveled pickup truck, delivering fruits and vegetables, only to have the produce sit unprotected on dirt floors. She showed families how to stack food and dishes

ELIZABETH JOSEPHINE BRAWLEY HUGHES

[1839~1926]

Josephine Hughes led the fight for women's suffrage in Arizona. Born in Meadville, Pennsylvania, on December 22, 1839, she headed west after marrying attorney Louis C. Hughes. Her arrival in Tucson was heralded by a determination to bring a semblance of civilization to the community. She introduced candles to her neighbors, had a cistern installed, put carpet on the floor of her adobe home, and grew lush grass in the front yard of her desert dwelling.

Josephine taught in Tucson's first public school for girls, helped organize the first Protestant (Presbyterian) church in Arizona, and later supported Tucson's Methodist Church, earning the title "Mother of Methodism in Arizona."

Louis Hughes became sole owner of the *Arizona Weekly Star* in 1879 (forerunner of the *Arizona Daily Star*), giving Josephine a platform from which to promote her campaigns, such as anti-gambling, removing Apaches from the territory, and her ongoing battle for temperance. As manager of the paper, she changed payday from Saturday to Monday to keep employees from starting the work week broke and hung over. She was also the first president of the Tucson chapter of the Women's Christian Temperance Union of Arizona.

When her husband became territorial governor in 1893, Josephine took over the newspaper. As one of the founders of the Arizona Suffrage Association, she freely used the paper to promote women's suffrage. Her son John became one of Arizona's first senators after statehood in 1912, introducing an amendment to the state constitution giving Arizona women the right to vote seven years before Congress passed the 19th Amendment.

Josephine moved to California after her husband's death and died at Hermosa Beach on April 22, 1926. A bronze plaque at the Arizona Capitol reads: "In Memoriam, E. Josephine Brawley Hughes, Wife of Governor L.C. Hughes and Mother of Hon. John T. Hughes: Mother of Methodism, Founder of the W.C.T.U. and Founder of the First Daily Newspaper in Arizona."

on boxes off the ground and how to wash dishes in clean water. She went to the council seeking money to build wooden floors in the hogans.

She insisted toilet facilities be built farther from houses and argued for sorely needed funds to improve water quality on the reservation. She taught women the benefits of canned meats and powdered milk, while advocating better health care for pregnant women and infants. She went to the departments of education in Arizona and New Mexico requesting that students be taught personal hygiene and disease prevention.

Annie instituted a dictionary of English/Navajo medical terms to provide a better understanding of doctor's instructions. She chaired the Alcoholism Committee and continued the efforts of her father to ban the sale of liquor on the reservation. And she took to the airwaves with a radio program focusing on health issues, broadcast in the Navajo language.

In 1959 Annie received the Indian Council Fire Achievement Award for her work in controlling the spread of tuberculosis. The Arizona Press Women's Club named her Woman of the Year for her community service, and the Arizona Public Health Association recognized her work in public health. She became the first woman to receive the Josephine B. Hughes Memorial Award for promoting the health and welfare of her people.

During the 1960s, the death rate among Navajo infants declined by 25 percent and the scourge of tuberculosis was reduced by 35 percent. The chief of the U.S. Public Health Service Division of Indian Health recognized Annie as the leader in improving the well-being of the Navajo. "No one individual has done more than Mrs. Wauneka to foster a wider understanding of health among the Indian people."

In 1963 she became the first Native American to receive the highest honor given to a civilian. President Lyndon B. Johnson awarded her the Presidential Medal of Freedom for her crusade in the "betterment of the health of her people... She succeeded in these efforts by winning the confidence of her people, and then by interpreting to them the miracles of modern medical science."

Annie became the voice of the Navajos in Washington D.C., speaking before Congress on numerous occasions. She always dressed in typical Navajo clothing—long tiered skirt topped by a plush velvet blouse, with a beautifully decorated large squash blossom necklace around her neck. When a congressman once told her to "quit playing Indian," her retort was typical of her brusque but effective manner. "Congressman...I didn't come here to talk about your clothes, so you ignore mine and let's talk legislation."

In the 1970s she joined a study on the status of Navajo women, for although they had power within their homes, they had no voice in the community. At a 1975 Southwestern Indian Women's Conference held in Window Rock, she urged women to move forward into the future while holding on to their Indian culture. "These changing times and changing attitudes can be detrimental to women," she said. "It's not just how men see us, but how we see ourselves. As we begin to demand expanded roles in the political, social, and cultural life of our people, we must not surrender our unique Indian identity. Otherwise we'll find ourselves asking, 'Mirror, mirror on the wall—who is this?' "

"Everyone is your family," she said. "Especially if you are a woman, everybody rests on your shoulders. Everybody walks with you."

In 1976 *Ladies Home Journal* selected Annie as Woman of the Year for her inspirational and educational leadership. She received an honorary doctoral degree in public health from the University of Arizona and an honorary doctorate in humane letters from the University of New Mexico. She was inducted into both the Arizona Women's Hall of Fame and the National Women's Hall of Fame. The Navajo Council declared her the Legendary Mother of the Navajo People.

At age eighty-three, Annie developed Alzheimer's disease and moved into a nursing home with George and several of their children. George died in 1994, and Annie followed him on November 19, 1997.

Navajo president Albert Hale called her "one of the great Navajo leaders. Her efforts in education, health, and the quest for justice and equality with our neighbors profoundly improved the lives of every one of us."

The year before her death, the University of Arizona awarded her an honorary doctor of law degree. Her grandson Milton Bluehouse Jr. accepted the award for her. "I didn't know she was famous until about my senior year in high school," he said. "Before that, I figured that she was just my grandmother. I thought, grandmothers do these things. They jump in their trucks and go everywhere."

WORTHY TO BE A JUDGE

Lorna Elizabeth Lockwood

[1903–1977]

As the somewhat stout, motherly looking woman headed into the court building, she was stopped by a guard who informed her she had to move her car as that parking spot was reserved for Arizona Supreme Court judges only. "It took some doing," laughed Lorna Lockwood, "but I finally persuaded him that I was entitled to it, even if I was a woman." In 1961, at the

LORNA ELIZABETH LOCKWOOD

age of fifty-eight, Lorna climbed the steps of the courthouse as the first woman to sit on the bench of the Arizona State Supreme Court. As a youngster, she had dreamed of becoming a lawyer and maybe someday a judge.

A native Arizonan, Lorna Elizabeth Lockwood was born in Douglas, Arizona, on March 24, 1903, the great-niece of Abraham Lincoln. In 1913 the family moved to Tombstone when her attorney father, Alfred C. Lockwood, was appointed superior court judge for Cochise County. Lorna graduated from Tombstone High School in 1920, but only after obeying her father, who insisted his daughter suspend her education for a year to learn the "domestic arts." Once she had conquered household duties, the judge wholeheartedly supported her efforts to break through glass ceilings not yet achieved by women.

Lorna graduated from the University of Arizona in 1923 and set her sights on a law degree, following in her father's footsteps. "There were only about two practicing woman lawyers in the state at the time," she recalled, "and my entrance into law school at U of A was much against the wishes of the Dean, who tried (without success) to talk me out of it." Following Nellie Bush as the second woman admitted to the law school, she was the first to graduate, in 1925, dispelling the objections of those who had long discouraged women from entering the field of law. As one judge contended back in 1875, "It would be shocking to man's reverence for womanhood that women should be permitted to mix professionally in all the nastiness of the world which finds its way into courts of justice."

Lorna found the judge's words prophetic when she discovered that no one would hire a woman lawyer, and the only jobs available were as legal secretary or law clerk. With her father now sitting on the bench of the Arizona State Supreme Court, she worked as his secretary until she acquired a job with a Phoenix law firm in the same capacity. In 1939 she partnered with Loretta Savage to open Phoenix's first all-woman law firm. Three years later the partnership dissolved—people were still hesitant to hire female attorneys.

During this time Lorna became active in the Democratic Party. She was elected as a precinct committeeperson and became the youngest president of the Democratic Women's Club. In 1939 she ran for and won a seat in the Arizona House of Representatives as a representative from Maricopa County. She was active on the Child Welfare Committee as well as in Public Health and Education, and her legal background provided her the opportunity to serve as vice-chair of the House Judiciary Committee. Reelected in 1941, she presided over the prestigious Judiciary Committee. During her first two terms in the House, she introduced seventeen bills, thirteen of them authored by her alone.

At the beginning of World War II, Lorna resigned her position and headed to Washington D.C. to work for a year as secretary to Arizona's lone member of the U.S. House of Representatives, John R. Murdock. Returning to Phoenix, she worked as an attorney for the wartime Office of Price Administration. After the war, she joined her father and brother-in-law in private practice.

Lorna entered politics again in 1947, winning her third term in the Arizona House of Representatives, but left the legislature in 1949 to accept the position of assistant attorney general for the State of Arizona.

In 1950 she sought a seat on the state's Superior Court representing Maricopa County. Always a little shy, she learned how to promote herself during this election. One of thirteen lawyers running for five seats on the court, she told her audiences to vote for the first candidate of their choice and for their second, third, and fourth selections. "All I ask is that you cast your fifth vote for me and give a woman a chance to prove herself on the bench in Arizona." On election day, Lorna garnered enough votes to land the fifth position on the bench, the first woman elected to Arizona's Superior Court.

"People were surprised," she said, "but the lawyers were the ones that were a little bit against it. They didn't think that a woman belonged on the bench. One of them said he knew I was a good lawyer, but he just didn't believe women should become judges... There weren't any real valid reasons given, just that a woman hadn't been there and therefore they shouldn't be."

Lorna quickly earned the reputation as a tough but fair judge, brooking no nonsense in her courtroom from attorneys who might think her easy prey. Antics from overly exuberant litigators usually resulted in a stiff fine and a stern lecture.

In 1954 she presided over the juvenile division of the court, making needed improvements in the treatment of children in the legal system. According to Lorna, "The juvenile court should consider not only the best welfare of the individual child brought before it but should also consider what is best for other persons including parents and society with which the child may be in conflict." She found the iron cells in the county juvenile detention facility so appalling she ordered them welded shut.

Her work with children extended beyond the courtroom. She was instrumental in founding the state's Big Sisters and Big Brothers organizations as well as the Girls' Ranch of Arizona. Her devotion to improving the lot of Arizona's youngsters took a toll on her health, however, and she left the juvenile bench in 1957, resuming her duties as a trial judge.

In 1960 Lorna was elected as the first woman to serve on the Arizona Supreme Court. She moved into the office once occupied by her father and resurrected his well-used desk, the one he had sat behind for eighteen years, most of those served as Arizona's chief justice.

In 1965 and again in 1970, Lorna Lockwood was selected as Arizona's chief justice, the first woman in the country to rise to the highest state judicial position.

When vacancies on the U.S. Supreme Court occurred in both 1965 and 1967, Arizona senator Carl Hayden put her name before President Lyndon B. Johnson as a possible candidate. Although President Johnson did not feel the country was ready to accept a woman on the Supreme Court, Lorna disagreed. "I don't think a woman should be denied a seat on the court just because she is a woman, and I don't think she should be given one just on the basis of being a woman either. The job is too important to be judged on this basis alone."

During her tenure on the Arizona Supreme Court, Lorna delivered more than five hundred opinions on cases that greatly affected the state as well as its populace. She authored a ruling rejecting the state's immunity from tort liability, determining "when the reason for a certain rule no longer exists, the rule itself should be abandoned." And although she did not render the renowned *Arizona v. Miranda* opinion, she was chief justice at the time and spoke up against the decision. "[I]f a person is caught committing a crime," she said, "he should not have to have the Miranda rights read to him."

"I have always prided myself in rendering decisions based on common sense, rather than strictly on legal precedent."

More than one attorney recognized her individuality. "In a tradition-encrusted profession in which novelty is not the order of the day," one remarked, "she has never been afraid of an idea because it was new."

During her run for a third term on the Supreme Court, she noted her lifelong tenure both in the legislature and the courts. "[I]t is clear to me that our courts are the key to preserving the moral strength of our community. Order and liberty have been my primary concerns. My work is not yet finished and I look forward enthusiastically to continuing service on the court."

"A Judge's Prayer" is sometimes credited as coming from Lorna's pen: "I pray that today I will have the knowledge to discover and the wisdom to clarify the legal issues; the ability to see, and the unbiased mind to recognize the true facts; the heart to know, and the gentleness to understand the human problems; the patience and logic to reach, and the courage to declare the just decision. All these things, Lord, I ask that at the close of this day my conscience may truly say, 'I am worthy to be a judge.' "

An advocate for women's rights, she denied being "a militant feminist, but I am terribly glad when women succeed." She served as mentor and friend to up-and-coming women attorneys and attended weekly luncheons where discussions ranged from legal issues to the nuances of dealing with male adversaries.

Through the years, Lorna held offices with numerous organizations, such as president and western regional director of the National Federation of Business and Professional Women's Clubs, president of the Soroptimist Club of Phoenix, president of the Arizona Judges Association, and sitting on the Governor's Commission on the Status of Women.

She received dozens of awards for breaking down barriers, allowing women attorneys to climb the professional ladder. In 1962 she was named Phoenix Professional Woman of the Year from the Arizona State Federation of Business and Professional Women. She accepted the Southern Pacific Coast Region of Hadassah Humanitarian Award in 1965, and the Woman of Achievement Award from the American Association of University Women in 1966, and was voted Outstanding Woman in the Field of Law by Who's Who of American Women in 1967. She was named Builder of a Greater Arizona in 1971 and awarded Phoenix Woman of the Year in 1974.

Her alma mater, the University of Arizona, honored her with the Arizona Distinguished Citizen Award and the Arizona Medallion of Merit. She became the first woman to receive the Arizona Alumni Achievement Award.

In 1975 ill health drove her from the bench. Lorna died on September 23, 1977. Accolades of her achievements poured from the courts. Then Chief Justice James Duke Cameron, commenting on her stature as the first woman to serve as chief justice in any state, declared "she achieved this position on merit. Lorna was a good judge and a tough judge when she had to be."

After her death, a group of women lawyers instituted the Lorna Lockwood Traveling Trophy, a svelte blonde Barbie doll dressed in a black robe. A plaque on the doll listed the names of Arizona women who had ascended to the judiciary. It was agreed that when the first Arizona woman was appointed to the U.S. Supreme Court, the trophy would be retired.

In 1981 Sandra Day O'Connor became the first woman elected to the U.S. Supreme Court. Crediting Lorna with giving her the drive to pursue her dreams, Justice O'Connor is now the proud possessor of the Lorna Lockwood Traveling Trophy. "Each position I held in Arizona was one that was attained by following a course made far more accessible because Lorna Lockwood had prepared the way by proving it could be done and done well by a woman," said Justice O'Connor. "As I look out my window each day, I am reminded of the contributions Lorna Lockwood made in opening doors for other women in the legal profession. Her kindly interest and encouragement of other women lives on in the work of those of us who were privileged to know her."

ACKNOWLEDGMENTS

Whenever I complete a writing project and look back at the wonderful people who assisted me, I am overwhelmed with the generosity and kindness with which others give of their time, talents, and ideas. Of those who provided me with information, guidance, and support, I wish to acknowledge publically the following individuals and institutions for making this project so much easier and so enjoyable.

Singer Katie Lee, almost ninety years of age when I met her in 2009, with the outlook of a twenty-year-old, opened her Jerome home and her larger-than-life heart as she reminisced about the early days of Hollywood and her futile fight to save Glen Canyon for future adventurers. I also spent a delightful afternoon with siblings Mary Rose Duffield and Christopher Carroll, grandniece and grandnephew of Sarah Sorin, walking through the old homestead in downtown Tucson as they remembered captivating anecdotes about their extraordinary relative.

Among administrators and members of establishments who helped with this project, I particularly want to acknowledge Eileen Warshaw, PhD, executive director of Tucson's Jewish History Museum, for introducing me to the accomplishments of Teresa Ferrin as well as other Jewish women who contributed so much to the growth of the Old Pueblo. Managing director of Prescott's Smoki Museum, Cynthia A. Gresser, as well as the museum staff, kindly allowed me access to artist Kate Cory's remarkable journal and artifacts. Richard D. Quartaroli, Northern Arizona University Cline Library special collections librarian, found elusive materials on several northern Arizona women I might have missed without his know-how. Scott Anderson at Sharlot Hall Museum provided me with numerous documents on central Arizona women. Deanna Beaver of the Parker Area Historical Society assisted me with the story of Nellie Bush.

Renowned sculptor Susan Kliewer graciously allowed me to use a photograph of her magnificent sculpture of Lozen, bringing the Apache warrior to life between these pages.

As a researcher, one of my favorite activities and pursuits is visiting historical institutions that save, restore, and provide access to thousands of archival materials, an integral part of the process of writing historical nonfiction. Along with the organizations mentioned above, I spent hundreds of hours at the Arizona Historical Society in Tucson and the University of Arizona Special Collections, and want to express my gratitude to those who aided me during my explorations and study.

To editors Caroline Cook and Jim Turner, I appreciate so much your editorial expertise.

I also want to recognize Bob Pugh of Trails to Yesterday Book Niche; Amy Hernandez, attorney-at-law; and historian Mary Melcher for their helpful contributions to my research. And to my husband and children, thank you for supporting me throughout the process of this absolutely fascinating adventure.

APPENDIX A

ARIZONA TIMELINE

1539	Fray Marcos de Niza and Estebanico become the first Europeans to enter Arizona.
1540–1542	Francisco Vasquez de Coronado led his Spanish expedition through Arizona, New Mexico, Texas, Oklahoma, and Kansas.
1687–1711	Father Eusebio Kino founded twenty-five missions, including San Xavier, Tumacacori, and Guevavi in what is now southern Arizona.
1751	The Pima Indian revolt killed more than 100 settlers and destroyed several missions.
1752	The first Spanish presidio (fort) was established in Arizona at Tubac.
1776	First Spanish troops begin to build Presidio San Agustín del Tucson.
1810–1821	The Mexican War for Independence freed Mexico from Spanish rule.
1821–1833	Mexican land grants created a cattle ranching industry in southern Arizona.
1822	The Santa Fe Trail opened, creating commerce between the United States and Mexico.
1846–1848	Mexico ceded all or part of California, New Mexico, Utah, Colorado, and New Mexico and Arizona with the Treaty of Guadalupe Hidalgo after the U.S.–Mexican War.
1848	Gold was discovered at Sutter's Mill. The Gila Trail through Arizona became a major route during the ensuing gold rush, bringing thousands of Americans through the area.

1854	President Franklin Pierce signed the Gadsden Purchase Treaty, adding southern Arizona to the United States.
1861	United States Army forts were abandoned as a result of the Civil War.
1862	The southern third of modern Arizona and New Mexico were admitted as the Confederate Territory of Arizona.
1862	On April 15th, Union and Confederate troops clashed at Picacho Peak, known as the westernmost battle of the Civil War.
1863	President Abraham Lincoln split New Mexico Territory in half, creating Arizona Territory with the first capital at Fort Whipple, near the rich gold fields around Prescott.
1864	More than 8,000 Navajos marched hundreds of miles to Bosque Redondo, New Mexico, in what became known as the Long Walk.
1868	The first post office in Phoenix is established; it was incorporated as a town in 1881.
1874	Martha Summerhayes, author of *Vanished Arizona,* accompanied her officer husband, Jack, to Arizona.
1877	Prospector Ed Schieffelin recorded the first Tombstone silver mining claims.
1880	Saint Mary's Hospital opened in Tucson, and the Southern Pacific Railroad arrived.
1881	The Southern Pacific Railroad completed the first transcontinental rail route across Arizona.
1884	On Sept. 4th, Geronimo surrendered to General Nelson Miles at Skeleton Canyon.
1886	Tempe Normal School opened; it became Arizona State University in 1958.
1889	The Arizona territorial capital moved to Phoenix.
1891	The University of Arizona opened in Tucson.
1902	Sarah Herring Sorin became the first woman admitted to the Arizona State Bar.
1910	Louisa and John Wetherill opened the Kayenta Trading Post on the Navajo Reservation.
1911	The Theodore Roosevelt Dam, first federal reclamation dam, was completed.
1912	Arizona became a state on February 14th. On November 5, women gained the right to vote in Arizona, eight years before the Nineteenth Amendment granted national women's suffrage.

1915	Frances Lillian Willard Munds became the first woman elected to the Arizona State Senate. Rachel Allen Berry became the first woman elected to the Arizona State House of Representatives.
1917	The interception and decoding of the Zimmerman telegram revealed that German diplomats offered to help Mexico regain Arizona and other lands ceded in the U.S.–Mexican War. It contributed to U.S. involvement in World War I.
1919	The Grand Canyon became a national park.
1922	Mary Elizabeth Jane Colter designed the Phantom Ranch tourist lodge at the bottom of the Grand Canyon.
1922	The Colorado River Compact is signed, distributing the river's water rights to Colorado, New Mexico, Utah, Wyoming, Nevada, Arizona, and California. Arizona Governor George W. P. Hunt refused to sign the agreement.
1928	The Sharlot Hall Museum opened in the original log governor's mansion in Prescott.
1929–1941	The Great Depression and New Deal programs such as the Works Projects Administration and Civilian Conservation Corps greatly affected Arizona's economy. The federal livestock reduction program on the Navajo Reservation strained government–Indian relations.
1936	Hoover Dam was completed on the Arizona–Nevada border, providing hydroelectric power and water to several Southwestern states.
1941–45	The United States employed members of several Arizona Indian tribes as code talkers in World War II.
1945	On February 23rd, Pima Indian Ira Hayes and four other U.S. Marines raised the American flag on Mount Suribachi, Iwo Jima, Japan.
1948	Arizona Indians obtain the right to vote through an Arizona Supreme Court decision in the case of *Harrison v. Laveen.*
1956	Construction began on the Glen Canyon Dam, completed in 1966. It flooded many canyons on the Colorado River and created Lake Powell.
1964	Senator Barry Goldwater became the Republican Party candidate for president.
1968	Congress approved the Central Arizona Project, which created pumps and canals to bring Colorado River water to central and southern Arizona. The project was completed in 1991.

1974	Raul Castro became the first Hispanic governor of Arizona.
1981	Arizona judge Sandra Day O'Connor became the first woman to serve on the United States Supreme Court.
1988	Governor Evan Mecham was impeached, and Secretary of State Rose Mofford of Globe, Arizona, became the first woman governor of Arizona.
1999	Arizona became the first state to have its top five elected offices held by women: Governor Jane Hull, Secretary of State Betsey Bayless, State Treasurer Carol Springer, Superintendent of Public Instruction Lisa Keegan, and Arizona Attorney General (and future governor) Janet Napolitano.

APPENDIX B

HONORING ARIZONA WOMEN WHO MADE HISTORY

Two of Arizona's most distinguished organizations, the Arizona Women's Hall of Fame and the Sharlot Hall Territorial Women's Memorial Rose Garden, have honored the following women from this book. For a complete list of inductees into these organizations, please go to the following web sites:

Arizona Women's Hall of Fame: **www.lib.az.us/awhof/**

Sharlot Hall Territorial Women's Memorial Rose Garden: **http://sharlot.org/ archives/rosegarden/**

★ ARIZONA WOMEN'S HALL OF FAME HONOREES ★

Our Arizona Women's Hall of Fame honorees have achieved greatness because they were determined. If they saw a need, they filled it. If they met an obstacle, they got around it. One way or another, they met the challenge.

—DR. REBA GRANDRUD, *Arizona Historian*

Mary Bier Bernard Aguirre	1844~1906
Cora Louise Boehringer	1878~1956
Eulalia "Sister" Collins Bourne	1892~1984
Nellie May Trent Bush	1888~1963
Nellie Cashman	circa 1845~1925
Mary Elizabeth Jane Colter	1869~1958

Doña Eulalia Elías González	1788~1865
Sharlot Mabridth Hall	1870~1943
Angela Hutchinson Hammer	1870~1952
Maie Bartlett Heard	1868~1951
Elizabeth Josephine Brawley Hughes	1839~1926
Lorna Elizabeth Lockwood	1903~1977
Nampeyo	circa 1860~1942
Mary Elizabeth Post	1841~1934
Polingaysi Qöyawayma (Elizabeth White)	1892~1990
Sicatuva (Viola Pelhame Jimulla)	1878~1966
Sarah Inslee Herring Sorin	1861~1914
Maria Luisa Legarra Urquides	1908~1944
Annie Dodge Wauneka	1910~1997
Louisa Wade Wetherill	1878~1945
Florence Brookhart Yount	1909~1988

★ SHARLOT HALL TERRITORIAL WOMEN'S MEMORIAL ROSE GARDEN ★

The Territorial Women's Memorial Rose Garden is dedicated to those women of Arizona who prepared the way for others. More than 400 women have been honored, representing nearly all occupations and ethnic backgrounds.

Nellie May Trent Bush	1888~1963
Kate Thomson Cory	1861~1958
Sharlot Mabridth Hall	1870~1943
Angela Hutchinson Hammer	1870~1952
Polingaysi Qöyawayma (Elizabeth White)	1892~1990
Sicatuva (Viola Pelhame Jimulla)	1878~1966
Elizabeth Hudson Smith	1879~1935
Louisa Wade Wetherill	1878~1945
Florence Brookhart Yount	1909~1988

RESOURCES AND SUGGESTED READING

Numerous interviews, newspapers, periodicals, and bibliographic files located in libraries, museums, and historical societies, plus a host of Internet sources were used in the research of this book. The following brief list of materials might be of interest to those wanting to pursue additional information about Arizona's remarkable women.

★ WOMEN OF THE LAND ★

Lozen
Aleshire, Peter. *Warrior Woman: The Story of Lozen, Apache Warrior and Shaman.* New York: St. Martin's Press, 2001.
Ball, Eve. *In the Days of Victorio: Recollections of a Warm Springs Apache.* Tucson: University of Arizona Press, 1970.
Buchanan, Kimberly Moore. *Apache Women Warriors.* El Paso: University of Texas Press, 1986.
Cremony, John C. *Life Among the Apaches.* New York: A. Roman & Company, 1868.
Robinson, Sherry. *Apache Voices: Their Stories of Survival as Told to Eve Ball.* Albuquerque: University of New Mexico Press, 2000.
Stockel, H. Henrietta. *Chiricahua Apache Women and Children: Safekeepers of the Heritage.* College Station: Texas A&M Press, 2000.

Larcena Ann Pennington Page Scott
Lockwood, Frank C. *Pioneer Portraits: Selected Vignettes.* Tucson: University of Arizona Press, 1968.
Roberts, Virginia Culin. *With Their Own Blood: A Saga of Southwestern Pioneers.* Ft. Worth: Texas Christian University Press, 1992.

Mary Bier Bernard Aguirre

Aguirre, Mary Bernard. "Spanish Trader's Bride." *The Westport Historical Quarterly* vol. 4, no. 3 (December 1968).

Gray, Annette. *Journey of the Heart: The True Story of Mamie Aguirre (1844–1906), A Southern Belle in the "Wild West."* Markerville, Alberta: Graytwest Books, 2001.

"The Journal of Mamie Bernard Aguirre." Kansas City, Missouri: *Jackson County Historical Society JOURNAL,* (Spring 1966).

Suderland, Nedra. "Mary Belle Bernard Aguirre: First Teacher at Tres Alamos." *The Cochise County Historical Journal,* vol. 28, no. 2 (Spring/Summer 1998).

Emma Louise Batchelor Lee French

Brooks, Juanita. *Emma Lee.* Logan: Utah State University Press, 1978.

———. *John Doyle Lee: Zealot, Pioneer–Builder, Scapegoat.* Glendale, California: Arthur H. Clark Company, 1961.

Kelly, Charles, ed. *Journals of John D. Lee, 1846–47 and 1859.* Salt Lake City: Western Printing Company, 1938.

Lee, John Doyle. *Mormonism Unveiled: Including the Remarkable Life and Confessions of the Late Mormon Bishop John D. Lee.* Albuquerque: Fierra Blanca Publications, 2001.

Measeles, Evelyn Brack. *Lees Ferry: A Crossing on the Colorado.* Boulder, Colorado: Pruett Publishing Company, 1981.

Ada Diefendorf Bass

Bass, Ada. Diary of Ada Bass. Arizona Historical Society, Tucson.

Leavengood, Betty. *Grand Canyon Women: Lives Shaped by Landscape.* Boulder, Colorado: Pruett Publishing Company, 1999.

Madsen, Lisa D. *The Grand Canyon Tourist Business of the W. W. Bass Family.* (master's thesis, University of New Mexico, 1980)

Mauer, Stephen G. *Solitude & Sunshine: Images of a Grand Canyon Childhood* (based on conversations with William G. Bass). Boulder, Colorado: Pruett Publishing Company, 1983.

Doña Eulalia Elías González

Brophy, Frank C. "The Romantic Saga of Four." *Arizona Highways,* 1966, accessed online at http://www.babacomariranch.com/pages/history.html.

Munson, Robert W. "Don Ignacio and Doña Eulalia Elias and the History of their Hacienda on the Babacomari: Camp Wallen." *The Cochise Quarterly* vol. 6, no. 1 (Spring 1976): 3-11.

Officer, James E. *Hispanic Arizona, 1536–1856.* Tucson: University of Arizona Press, 1987.

Wilson, John P. *Islands in the Desert: A History of the Uplands of Southeastern Arizona.* Albuquerque, University of New Mexico Press, 1995.

★ WOMEN WHO HEALED AND SAVED ★

Sisters of St. Joseph of Carondelet

Ames, Sister Aloysia, C.S.J. *The St. Mary's I Knew*. Tucson: St. Mary's Hospital, 1970.

Bryne, Leo G., and Sister Alberta Cammack, C.S.J. "A Heritage of Loving Service: The Sisters of St. Joseph of Carondelet in Tucson." Accessed at http://parentseyes.arizona.edu/carondelet/heritage_toc.html.

McMahon, Sister Thomas Marie, C.S.J., B.A. *The Sisters of St. Joseph of Carondelet: Arizona's Pioneer Religious Congregation, 1870–1890*. (master's thesis, St. Louis University, 1952)

The Trek of the Seven Sisters. Diary of Sister Monica Corrigan. n.d. Accessed at http://parentseyes.arizona.edu/carondelet/trekofthesevensisters_toc.html

Teresita Urrea

Griffith, James S. *Folk Saints of the Borderlands: Victims, Bandits & Healers*. Tucson: Rio Nuevo Publishers, 2003.

Holden, William Curry. *Teresita*. Owings Mills, Maryland: Stemmer House Publishers, 1978.

Theresa Marx Ferrin

Bloom Family. University of Arizona Special Collections.

Winston-Macauley, Marnie. *"Yiddish Mamas": The Truth about the Jewish Mother*. Kansas City: Andrews McMeel Publishing, 2007.

St. Katharine (Catherine Hookey Drexel)

Baldwin, Lou. *Saint Katharine Drexel: Apostle to the Oppressed*. Philadelphia: The Catholic Standard and Times, 2000.

Burton, Katharine. *The Golden Door: The Life of Katharine Drexel*. New York: P. J. Kenedy & Sons, 1957.

Duffy, Sister Consuela Marie, S.B.S. *Katharine Drexel: A Biography*. Cornwell Heights, Pennsylvania: Sisters of the Blessed Sacrament, 1966.

Florence Brookhart Yount

Palmer, Verina E. "Dr. Florence Yount: A Determined Woman and Physician." *The Prescott Daily Courier*, January 16, 1989.

Simpson, Claudette. "Florence Yount Recalls Medical Career." *The Prescott Daily Courier: Days Past*, March 5, 1985.

Yount, Florence B., M.D. "Hospitals in Prescott." Undated speech given by Dr. Yount. On file at Sharlot Hall Museum, Prescott, Arizona.

———. "The Good Old Days." Undated speech given by Dr. Yount. On file at Sharlot Hall Museum, Prescott, Arizona.

Katherine Ruth Beard

Armstrong, Hart. *A Life Poured Out: The Life and Ministry of Katherine Beard*. Wichita: Christian Communications, Inc., 1988.

Carlson, Vada F. "Missionary to the Navajos." *Desert Magazine* vol. 20, no. 7 (July 1957).

★ WOMEN ENTREPRENEURS ★

Sarah Bowman

Elliott, J. F. "The Great Western: Sarah Bowman, Mother and Mistress to the U.S. Army." *Journal of Arizona History* vol. 30, no. 1 (Spring 1989).

Moynahan, Jay. *Sarah Bowman: Pioneer Madam.* Spokane: Chickadee Publishing, 2004.

Sandwich, Brian. *The Great Western: Legendary Lady of the Southwest.* El Paso: Texas Western Press, 1991.

Nellie Cashman

Chaput, Don. *Nellie Cashman and the North American Mining Frontier.* Tucson: Westernlore Press, 1995.

Ledbetter, Suzann. *Nellie Cashman: Prospector and Trailblazer.* El Paso: Texas Western Press, 1993.

Rochlin, Harriet. "The Amazing Adventures of a Good Woman." *Journal of the West* vol. 12, no. 2 (April 1972).

Louisa Wade Wetherill

Comfort, Mary Apolline. *Rainbow to Yesterday: The John and Louisa Wetherill Story.* New York: Vantage Press, 1980.

Gillmor, Frances. *A Biography of John and Louisa Wetherill.* (master's thesis, University of Arizona, 1931)

Gillmor, Frances, and Louisa Wade Wetherill. *Traders to the Navajos: The Story of the Wetherills of Kayenta.* New York: Houghton Mifflin Company, 1934.

Wyman, Leland C. *The Sandpaintings of the Kayenta Navajo: An Analysis of the Louisa Wade Wetherill Collection.* Albuquerque: University of New Mexico Press, 1952.

Elizabeth Hudson Smith

Cleere, Jan. "Hostess to the West." *Arizona Highways* vol. 77, no. 10 (October 2001).

Pry, Mark. *The Town on the Hassayampa.* Wickenburg, Arizona: Desert Caballeros Western Museum, 1997.

Taylor, Quintard. *In Search of the Racial Frontier: African Americans in the American West, 1528–1990.* New York: W.W. Norton & Company, 1998.

The Right Side Up Town on the Upside Down River. Wickenburg, Arizona: Maricopa County Historical Society, Las Señoras de Socorro, 1975.

Angela Hutchinson Hammer

Joy, Betty E. Hammer, *Angela Hutchinson Hammer: Arizona's Pioneer Newspaperwoman.* Tucson: University of Arizona Press, 2005.

Anna Magdalena Box Neal

Bentz, Donald N. "William and Anna Neal of Oracle and the Mountain View Hotel" *Oracle Historian,* (Summer 1982).

Harris, Richard E. *First 100 Years: A History of Arizona Blacks.* Apache Junction: Relmo Publishers, 1983.

Marriott, Barbara. *Annie's Guests: Tales from a Frontier Hotel.* Tucson: Catymatt Productions, 2000.

Wilson, George Stone. "Saga of Oracle Mountain Cow Town," (1887–1957). *Arizona Cattlelog,* (August 1964).

★ WOMEN WHO EDUCATED ★

Mary Elizabeth Post

Boehringer, C. Louise. "Mary Elizabeth Post—High Priestess of Americanization." *Arizona Historical Review* vol. 2, no. 2 (July 1929).

Gordon, Ruth Leedy. *Portrait of a Teacher: Mary Elizabeth Post and Something of the Times in Which She Lived, 1841–1934.* Copyright 1990 by Janet Gordon-Roach, David G. Gordon, and James H. Gordon Jr.

Polingaysi Qöyawayma (Elizabeth White)

Qöyawayma, Polingaysi (Elizabeth Q. White), as told to Vada F. Carlson. *No Turning Back: A Hopi Woman's Struggle to Live in Two Worlds.* Albuquerque: University of New Mexico Press, 1964.

Eulalia "Sister" Collins Bourne

Bourne, Eulalia. *Ranch Schoolteacher.* Tucson: University of Arizona Press, 1974.

———. *Woman in Levi's.* Tucson: University of Arizona Press, 1967.

Rebecca Huey Dallis

Dallis, Rebecca H. *A Critical Survey of Extra-Curricular Activities in Negro Secondary Schools.* (master's thesis, University of Arizona, 1935)

Tracy, Cindy. Meeting Mrs. Dallis. *Pinal Ways,* (Summer 2000).

Maria Luisa Legarra Urquides

Gonzalez, Elizabeth Quiros. *The Education and Public Career of Maria L. Urquides: A Case Study of a Mexican American Community Leader.* (doctoral dissertation, University of Arizona, 1986)

Cora Louise Boehringer

Brown, Wynne. *More than Petticoats: Remarkable Arizona Women.* Guilford, Connecticut: TwoDot, an imprint of the Globe Pequot Press, 2003.

Lo Vecchio, Janolyn. "C. Louise Boehringer: Arizona's First Lady of Education." Arizona Historical Society Convention Paper, April 28, 2000.

Nilson, Alleen Pace, Margaret Ferry and L.J. Evans, collectors and editors. *Dust in Our Desks: Territory Days to the Present in Arizona Schools.* Tempe: Arizona State University College of Education, 1985.

★ WOMEN OF THE ARTS ★

Martha Dunham Summerhayes

Summerhayes, Martha. *Vanished Arizona.* Lincoln: University of Nebraska Press, 1979. Reprint of 2nd ed. (1911) published by Salem Press, Salem, Massachusetts.

Sharlot Mabridth Hall

Hall, Sharlot M. *A Diary of a Journey Through Northern Arizona in 1911: Sharlot Hall on the Arizona Strip.* C. Gregory Crampton, ed. Prescott: Sharlot Hall Museum Press, 1999. Originally published by Northland Publishing Company, Flagstaff, Arizona, 1975.

———. *Cactus and Pine: Songs of the Southwest,* 3rd ed., rev. Prescott: Sharlot Hall Museum, 1989.

———. *Poems of a Ranch Woman.* Compiled by Josephine Mackenzie. With a biography by Charles Franklin Parker. Prescott: Sharlot Hall Historical Society of Arizona, 1953.

Maxwell, Margaret F. *A Passion for Freedom: The Life of Sharlot Hall.* Tucson: University of Arizona Press, 1982.

Weston, James J. "Sharlot Hall: Arizona's Pioneer Lady of Literature." *Journal of the West* vol. 4, no. 4 (October 1965).

Wright, Nancy Kirkpatrick, ed. *Sharlot Herself: Selected Writing of Sharlot Hall.* Prescott: Sharlot Hall Museum Press, 1992.

Mary Elizabeth Jane Colter

Avadenka, Lynne. *The Uncommon Perspective of M. E. J. Colter.* Huntington Woods, Michigan: Land Marks Press, 1992.

Berke, Arnold. *Mary Colter: Architect of the Southwest.* New York: Princeton Architectural Press, 2002.

Grattan, Virginia L. *Mary Colter: Builder Upon the Red Earth.* Grand Canyon: Grand Canyon Natural History Association, 1992. First printed by Northland Publishing, 1980.

Nampeyo

Anthony, Alexander E., Jr. *Nampeyo of Hano and Five Generations of her Descendants.* Albuquerque: Published in conjunction with an exhibit at Adobe Gallery, August 14–September 5, 1983.

Blair, Mary Ellen, and Laurence Blair. *The Legacy of a Master Potter: Nampeyo and Her Descendents.* Tucson: Treasure Chest Books, 1999.

Bunzel, Ruth L. *The Pueblo Potter: A Study of Creative Imagination in Primitive Art.* New York: Dover Publications, Inc., 1972. (Unabridged republication of the work originally published by Columbia University Press, New York, 1929.)

Kramer, Barbara. *Nampeyo and Her Pottery.* Tucson: University of Arizona Press, 1996.

Kate Thomson Cory

Johnson, Ginger. *Kate T. Cory: Artist of Arizona 1861–1958.* Privately published, October 1996.

Loscher, Tricia. "Kate Thomson Cory: Artist in Hopiland." *The Journal of Arizona History* vol. 43, no. 1 (Spring 2002).

Wright, Barton, Marnie Gaede, and Marc Gaede. *The Hopi Photographs: Kate Cory: 1905–1912.* La Canada, California: Chaco Press, 1986.

Katie Lee

Leavengood, Betty. *Grand Canyon Women: Lives Shaped by Landscape.* Boulder, Colorado: Pruett Publishing Company, 1999.

Lee, Katie. *All My Rivers are Gone: A Journey of Discovery Through Glen Canyon.* Boulder, Colorado: Johnson Books, 1998.

———. "Sabino on the Rocks." *Journal of Arizona History* vol. 49, no. 4 (Winter 2008).

Maie Bartlett Heard

Heard Museum web site. Accessed at www.heard.org.

Luke, Timothy W. "The Heard Museum." *Inventing the Southwest: The Fred Harvey Company and Native American Art.* Accessed at http://www.cddc.vt.edu/tim/tims/tim464.htm.

★ WOMEN OF THE LAW ★

Sarah Inslee Herring Sorin

Janitch, Danielle. "Sarah Herring Sorin: Arizona's First Woman Attorney." *Women in the Law.* Stanford Law School, April 6, 2001. Accessed at http://www.law.stanford.edu/library/ womenslegalhistory/papers0203/Sorin_DJanitch-S01.pdf.

Kasper, Jacquelyn. "Arizona's First Woman Lawyer: Sarah Herring Sorin." Tucson: Arizona Historical Society convention paper, 1999.

———. "Practicing Law in Territorial Arizona in a Skirt: The Tucson Years of Arizona's First Woman Lawyer, Sarah Herring Sorin." Tucson: Arizona Historical Society convention paper, 2006.

Sicatuva (Viola Pelhame Jimulla)

Barnett, Franklin, *Viola Jimulla: The Indian Chieftess.* Publication approved by Prescott Yavapai Indians, Prescott, Arizona. n.d.

Braatz, Timothy. *Surviving Conquest: A History of the Yavapai Peoples.* Lincoln: University of Nebraska Press, 2003.

Savage, Pat. *One Last Frontier: A Story of Indians, Early Settlers and Old Ranches of Northern Arizona.* New York: Exposition Press, 1964.

Nellie May Trent Bush

Beaver, Deanna. "Nellie T. Bush—'One of a Kind.' " Unpublished manuscript at Parker (Arizona) Area Historical Society.

Kelly, Rita Mae, ed. *Women and the Arizona Political Process.* Tempe: University Press of America, Inc., 1988.

Osselaer, Heidi J. *Winning Their Place: Arizona Women in Politics, 1883–1950.* Tucson: University of Arizona Press, 2009.

Annie Dodge Wauneka

Gridley, Marion E. *American Indian Women.* New York: Hawthorn Books, Inc., 1974.

Niethammer, Carolyn. *I'll Go and Do More: Annie Dodge Wauneka, Navajo Leader and Activist.* Lincoln: University of Nebraska Press, 2001.

Lorna Elizabeth Lockwood

Chanin, Abe, with Mildred Chanin. *This Land These Voices: A Different View of Arizona History in the Words of Those Who Lived It.* Flagstaff, Arizona: Northland Press, 1977.

Jacobs, Thomas A., and Nancy L. Matter. *Justice was a Lady: A Biography of the Public Life of Lorna E. Lockwood.* Unpublished manuscript copyright 1985 by Thomas A. Jacobs, available at the Arizona Historical Society.

Osselaer, Heidi J. *Winning Their Place: Arizona Women in Politics 1883–1950.* Tucson: University of Arizona Press, 2009.

Elizabeth Josephine Brawley Hughes

Bohl, Sarah. "Arizona's Progressive Women Editor: Josephine Brawley Hughes." Arizona Historical Society Convention Paper, 2006.

Morales, Melissa. "Why Early Twentieth Century Women Made their Splash in Arizona Politics." Accessed at www.ic.arizona.edu/ic/mcbride/ws200/mora-twen.htm.

PHOTO CREDITS

Archives of the Sisters of the Blessed Sacrament: page 53

Arizona Historical Society/Tucson: #11997, page 23; #341, front cover and page 28; #62524, page 37; #17674, page 47; #22073, page 77; #7208, page 91; #58D, page 101; #90563, front cover and page 112; #17431, front cover and page 157

Arizona State Library, Archives and Public Records, History and Archives Division, Phoenix: #04-7800, page 82; #97-8514, front cover and page 121; #98-8889, page 140; #04-7811, page 160; #98-9900, page 167; #93-9900, page 170; #97-7013, page 176; #94-0662, front cover and page 173; #97-7934, page 11; #02-9514, page 16; #97-7506, page 68; #97-6236, page 109

Dr. Hart R. Armstrong and Christian Communications Inc.: page 48

Casa Grande Valley Historical Society: front cover and page 107

First Congregational Church of Prescott: front cover and page 144

Grand Canyon National Park Museum Collection #16952: page 131

The Hopi Tribe, Snow, Milton: page 96

Katie Lee Archives: page 148

Susan Kliewer, sculptor: page 6

Northern Arizona University, Cline Library: Nichols, Tad, page 136; Young, Stuart M., page 73

Rembrandt Photography: page 198

Sharlot Hall Museum: pages 56, 126

Southwest Collection/Special Collections Library, Texas Tech University, Lubbock, Texas: page 42

University of Arizona Special Collections: front cover bottom right

ABOUT THE AUTHOR

JAN CLEERE graduated magna cum laude from Arizona State University West at the age of "50-something." She writes extensively about the desert Southwest, its unique characters, creatures, and vegetation. Her work appears in numerous regional publications including *Arizona Highways, Persimmon Hill Magazine, Phoenix Woman, Tucson Guide Quarterly, The Desert Leaf, Chronicle of the Old West,* and *Arizona Garden.*